NO LONG
SEATTL

S'Mother

The Story of a Man, His Mom, and the Thousands of
Altogether Insane Letters She's Mailed Him

Adam Chester

ABRAMS IMAGE
New York

Editor: David Cashion
Designer: Topos Graphics
Production Manager: Alison Gervais

Library of Congress Cataloging-in-Publication Data

Chester, Adam.
 S'mother : the story of a man, his mom, and the thousands of altogether
insane letters she's mailed him / Adam Chester.
     p. cm.
 Includes bibliographical references and index.
 ISBN 978-0-8109-9645-8 (alk. paper)
 1. Mothers and sons—United States—Correspondence—Humor. 2. Adult
children—Family relationships—United States—Humor. I. Title.
 HQ755.86.C44 2011
 306.874'3092—dc22
                        2010032491

ISBN 978-0-8109-9645-8

Copyright © 2011 Adam Chester
Published in 2011 by Abrams Image, an imprint of ABRAMS. All rights reserved. No portion of this book
may be reproduced, stored in a retrieval system, or transmitted in any form or by any means, mechanical,
electronic, photocopying, or otherwise, without written permission from the publisher.

Printed and bound in USA
10 9 8 7 6 5 4 3 2 1

Abrams Image books are available at special discounts when purchased in quantity for premiums and
promotions as well as fundraising or educational use. Special editions can also be created to specification.
For details, contact specialmarkets@abramsbooks.com, or the address below.

THE ART OF BOOKS SINCE 1949
115 West 18th Street
New York, NY 10011
www.abramsbooks.com

This book is dedicated to everyone who *has* a mother, who *knows* a mother, who *is* a mother, who will *be* a mother, or just likes to say the word "Mother."

That cat Joan is a baaaaad mother—
(*Shut your mouth!*)
But I'm talkin' about Adam's Mom.
> —Theme from *Shaft*, Variation #1

God came to me last night and told me your purpose for
being here. I am going to help you write a new book.
> —Annie Wilkes in Stephen King's *Misery*

Foreword

Mothers. They are known by many names: Mama, Ma, Mommy, Mumzy, Mamasita, or, that old standard in my house when I was growing up, "The most whacked-out woman I've ever been humbled to claim as my very own relative who has single-handedly tried to jeopardize any and every relationship I've ever had." Aaaaah. Just writing that makes me feel better. You've heard that old adage "You can't live with 'em . . ."? Well amen to that, brother. It's also my firm belief that mothers should provide immediate family members with ample warning bcFORE just "popping by" for a few minutes, or face serious consequences.

I know. You're thinking I've got issues. Fact is, when my wife and I moved into our house, it was my WIFE who didn't want to give my mother our new address. And for a while, it was peaceful. I was free— free, I tell you! No, I'm not being cruel, trust me. I should say this now, so we all feel better about each other: I eventually caved and told my mother where we lived, OK? Something about her wanting to see her grandkids . . . I don't know. (*I think she's just using them as a ruse to keep tabs on my life, but my shrink says that might be a tad extreme.*) Although

I do love and care about her (*as most sons who have been humiliated by their mothers most every day of their lives would*), I've got PLENTY of reasons why I keep my distance. Most of which I tossed into a large box I hid in the corner of my garage for close to thirty years of my life. (*You'll know more about that soon enough.*) What it all boils down to is the simple fact that my mother is insane. Not dangerously insane, I'll grant you, but nonetheless completely bats.

Throughout my entire life, my friends would say, "Come on, Adam. Your mom's not nuts. She's just your typical overprotective Jewish mother." But I knew the truth. I knew there must have been some medical term for her, and I realized we had some serious boundary issues that had nothing to do with our proximity.

When I think about all the incidents involving her that I managed to live through . . . I remember (*insert heavenly harp arpeggio here*) all the way back to . . .

My first year of junior high school in Miami Beach. It was a typical hot and humid school day. I remember it like it was yesterday because I relive this day almost every day of my life. I had a lot of friends. I also had a crush on a beautiful girl in my seventh-grade class; my first crush. Her name was Sara. She was everything a thirteen-year-old boy could want in a girl: She was pretty, she was popular, and she was a girl.

There I was, getting dressed with all my seventh-grade pals in the boys' locker room, as Phys Ed was just over. We were all joking around and laughing about stuff when suddenly I could hear that voice coming toward me from the distance. "Adam . . . ? Adam . . . ?" Could it be? No. Why would *she* be at school in the middle of the day? I tried to rationalize this as my heart started beating really fast. The voice was drawing closer . . . "Aaaaadaaaammmmm?" No doubt about it now. It was *her*. All the guys were panicking to get dressed in time. (*In time for what?*) The room became a blur as everyone was moving fast to at least cover up. But it was too late because she was . . .

I could see that my mother was carrying something as she stepped into the boys' locker room. No. (*Yes.*) No. (*Why?*) It was my sweater.

And I remember at that moment she looked completely at peace with what she was about to do. As I lifted my slightly watery gaze to look past her, I could see she was not alone. She was shadowed closely by our school coach (*who didn't know what the hell was going on*), who was followed by Sara, who was followed by anyone and everyone who had ever lived in South Florida during the 1970s. The room settled down for one final peaceful moment as my mother stepped into the spotlight, clutched what looked to me like a bullhorn, and proclaimed, "You forgot to bring your sweater. It's going to rain today!"

Those were the last words I heard as the room went black.

Seriously, don't feel bad. I came home that day and retreated to my bedroom, where I shut the door, stared at the various Elton John posters covering my wall, and fell asleep listening to "Someone Saved My Life Tonight." In the end, the whole experience made for a great icebreaker with classmates, co-workers, prospective dates, and psychologists. Where was my father during all of this? When I was eight years old, he lost his three-year battle with pancreatic cancer at the age of forty-three. Being the only child, I had to assume his place as the man of the house. My mom thought it'd be a good idea for us to move closer to her folks in Florida. Thus, my education from the fourth grade through high school took place in Miami Beach.

My mother never wanted to be a single mom, but like so many other women, she was thrust into that situation at a very young age. And in my humble opinion, I think my mother did a great job raising me. She may not have always behaved rationally, but she was there for me. All the time. Everywhere. 24/7. Without fail. Alienating most every other human being I'd ever seen her encounter. In fact, if those Christmas carolers are reading this right now, please accept my sincerest apologies on her behalf. I really thought you sang quite beautifully. You remember. Back in Princeton, New Jersey, on a snowy Christmas morning . . . I was only seven years old, and I'd been up all night with a flu and fever, and well, you understand. I guess you just picked the wrong apartment doorstep to stand on. I remember you all running like hell from my mother when she chased you down the block with a long broomstick, convinced you were disturbing my sleep. You guys were good.

And to that really nice elementary school bus driver: If *you're* reading this, I'm sorry about that day when my mother forced you off your own bus, only to allow my grandmother the opportunity to take it for a spin around the block a few times. I'm sure you were wondering what the hell was happening in that half hour or so, and I do hope if my mother hadn't already told you that day, this helps: You see, the brakes had to be tested before I was allowed to ride. All good! Thumbs up.

And if my mother is reading this right now, please stop asking me when someone I know in the entertainment industry will be turning this story into a feature film. I have no connections to Leonardo Di-Caprio, and Steven Spielberg is a very busy man.

I had no choice but to accept my costarring role in my life's popular, nontelevised reality show, *Adam's Mom*, as best I could. During my last year of high school, I started to contemplate where to escape to for college. There were only two requirements:

It had to have a good music school and—more important— the school had to meet my GET-ME-AS-FAR-AWAY-FROM-MY-MOTHER-AS-YOU-POSSIBLY-CAN distance minimum. I got brochures for schools in Italy, Australia, Iceland . . . any place that sounded really far. Eventually, I settled on just moving across my own country when I got accepted into the music school at the University of Southern California. And pretty soon I was thinking that California was the place I ought to be, so I loaded up my car and I moved to USC. But as I looked in my rearview mirror and saw my mother waving good-bye, I knew that this was far from over.

Driving that distance of 2,731 miles helped me feel like an independent adult male for the first time in my life. With each new time zone I entered, my past felt farther and farther away.

Soon after arriving at school, the letters started coming. Not the typical "How are things going?" and "Miss you" type of letters that came to many students who were away from their families. Oh, no.

These were different from the get-go. Much less mainstream. Less predictable. Less normal. The letters I got asked odd questions. Some would tell me strange stories about people I had never heard of, while others would warn me of perilous events. I'm quite sure that anyone else would have ignored these letters or destroyed them altogether. But not me. Even when they pushed me over the edge, I tossed them into that (*soon to be large*) box I kept hidden from every other form of life I knew. I couldn't take the chance that they'd be discovered by anyone. Not counting the ones I destroyed out of pure frustration, I managed to collect more than 1,000 letters. Some of which have remained in that box, unopened to this very day.

A little over a year ago, I walked into my garage and just stood there and stared at that box, wondering what was inside. I must have remained frozen for a good thirty minutes before reaching down to pick it up. I carried it into my family's new house, and carefully placed it down on the floor in the middle of the living room. It looked so out of place, so used. The plastic was torn on one side of the box from the weight, but it managed to hold itself together. My wife couldn't believe it, but she knew what I had in mind. It was time. Time to reveal what sort of peculiarities I was being sent in the mail to that very day, and collecting in that box for all these years.

Now you're probably thinking, Who in this day and age (*and in their right mind*) still uses the United States Postal Service to communicate with others? Why not use a phone or e-mail? Well, first of all, my mother is a little old-fashioned. She wants nothing to do with computers. She doesn't own one, nor will she think about learning how to use one, so corresponding with her via the Internet is out of the question. And while there have been some terrifically embarrassing phone messages from her over the years, nothing compares to her letters. They allow her the proper space to better detail the never-ending array of fears, warnings, and curious discoveries that forever cloud her brain. For my mother, her letters are therapy. For me, her letters document my reasons for therapy.

1.
Mom 101

Eighteen. I was a decent-looking USC college freshman with a bad-ass Cutlass Supreme, my very own upright piano from childhood that I had shipped directly to my dorm, three new roommates, a full schedule of music classes, and a view of the Hollywood sign from my living room window. For a guy who'd never been to sleepaway camp (*or to ANY camp for that matter, or allowed to sleep over at a nearby relative's house, or a friend's house . . . OK . . . maybe once, but . . .*), this was the life!

The two-bedroom, one-bath dorm was on the seventh floor of an on-campus, fourteen-story building known as Webb Tower. This was the first place I was to form one of my many long-term relationships with a mailbox. This particular one had a satin-brass finish, and was built into a large conglomeration of similar mailboxes located in the lobby. I was the main proprietor of the box known to me as 711. Two of my roommates were from California, so they weren't far enough away from home to warrant an abundance of mail. My other roommate was a tough guy from Boston who was not a member of any Let's-Keep-in-Touch Club. So the doggone box was mine.

The first letter I received from my mother was this postcard:

September 27, 1981
Dear Adam—
Another view from San Francisco—If you go here—
make sure you bring your winter coat—you'll need it.—
gets very cold—
Love,
Mom

A typical motherly warning, you say? Nothing off the deep end? Perhaps . . . but it would have been a wee bit embarrassing if one of my roommates were to have read it. I don't remember my mother ever even going to San Francisco, but it would stand to reason that the only thing she'd have to tell me about it was its arctic weather and how I might avoid hospitalization from frostbite when visiting.

Then this came:

October 3, 1981
Dear Adam,
You never have time to talk on the phone. Are you
meeting any nice girls?
    Make sure you dry your dishes before you put
them away.
Love,
Mom

San Fr
The fog,
backgroun.
breathless.
6407-D
Pub. by Sm

What the . . . ? It was strange, but I let it go. For what it's worth, I hung on to the letter. I never asked my mother what she meant by those words. Perhaps she'd just dropped a dish and had it on her mind when she put the pen to the pad. Maybe she was just kidding around (*oh, sure*). Or maybe she was convinced that somehow if she didn't warn me, a wet serving tray would end up doing me in. Then, I received this. Believe me, I'm not leaving anything out. What you see is all there was:

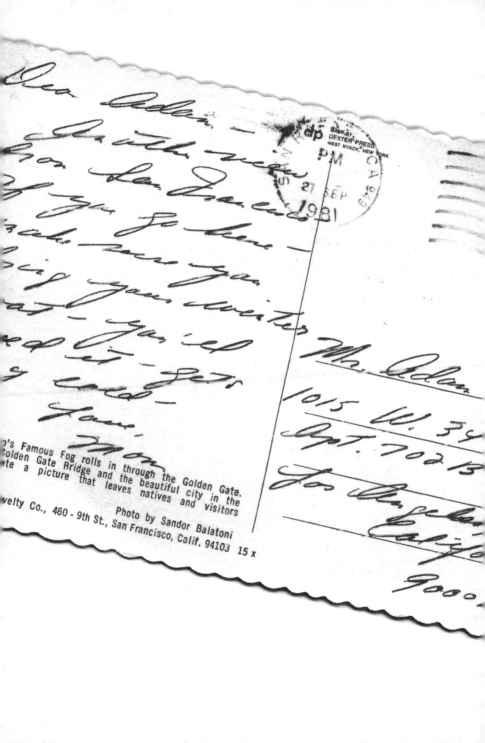

Dear Adam —

Sure wish
you were here —

[handwritten message, largely illegible]

Love,
Mom

's Famous Fog rolls in through the Golden Gate.
olden Gate Bridge and the beautiful city in the
te a picture that leaves natives and visitors
                    Photo by Sandor Balatoni
velty Co., 460 - 9th St., San Francisco, Calif. 94103 15 x

MADE BY
DEXTER PRESS
WEST NYACK," NEW YORK

27 SEP
PM
1981

Mr. Adam
1015 W. 34
Apt. 702 B
Los Angeles
California
900

Tues.

Adam—

Don't have anything to do with your paternal grandmother—

Love,

Mom

And the gloves are off, ladies and gentlemen! While there is a
backstory to her demand, to see it on paper like that always makes
me shake my head in pure disbelief. You see, at my mother's insis-
tence, I had not spoken to anyone on my father's side of the family
since the day he died in 1971. I guess she sent me that little reminder
letter in case I forgot Adam's Mom's RULE NUMBER ONE: Do not
have ANYTHING to do with my evil relatives in New Jersey.

It all started in 1971, when my mother received a letter from her
brother-in-law (*my uncle*) stating that now that his brother (*my
father*) was dead, they (*my evil relatives*) wanted nothing to do with us
(*my mother*) ever again. Now, correct me if I'm wrong, but I've heard
that in some (*normal*) families, when a person dies, the mother,

brother, and sister-in-law of said person don't write a letter cutting
off the rest of their grieving family. Not so much with this gang.

To say my mother had a vile relationship with that side of the family is the understatement of all time-and-space continuums. They
all passionately loathed each other, if for no other reason than the
claim of ownership both sides felt they had over my father. I believe
my mother felt my father was HERS, and this pissed my dad's family
off. And vice versa. In the tug-of-war between his family and his wife
that he was forced to partake in, my father chose his wife. (*Why does
this sound so familiar to me?*) Because of their rift, all of us first cousins
never got to know each other. Oh, well. *C'est la vie.* Who needs family when you're growing up? I knew that somewhere down the line,
later in life, I'd have to fix the whole damn mess, but first things first.
I knew the moment that particular warning letter from my mother
arrived that it was my duty, my calling, my obligation, to become the
first and only official curator of all things Adam's Mom. (*If for no other reason than to make people feel better about their own mothers.*)

I'm a positive kind of guy. I adapt well to new situations, love
meeting new people, and had no issues with having moved so far
away from my mother for a single second. (*Duh.*) Now, imagine my
surprise when I received a last will and testament in the mail from
her. Was she gravely ill and not telling me about it? Was she just being uncharacteristically responsible? I soon learned it was neither.
No, no. Last wills were to become one of the main recurring themes
in our correspondence. If it wasn't the will itself, it would be a list of
her various insurance policies, retirement funds, and possessions
that made up the boatload I was to inherit, if and when anything ever
happened to her. The odd thing is that the list rarely differed from
letter to letter. It consisted of the same policies and the same benefit
amounts, while offering my mother the same amount of relief (*each
time*) to finally have it all in writing. Yet when that first one came . . .
sure, I got a little nervous. I had never seen a will before. What's
wrong? Why the will? I guess every college student should have a
copy to pull out from their school locker. Just in case.

Sunday

Adam—

Enclosed is a copy of my latest Will.

Love,

Mom

I decided to look around campus for other forms of life who were receiving wills in the mail. Remember: This was the era before the Internet, cell phones, and home computers. If you wanted to make a friend, you had to get off your feet. Perhaps there was someone else out there in the big bad world with a family (*read: mother*) like mine! I had been looking for a fraternity to pledge, even though I am NOT your typical frat boy. I hadn't had my hair cut short since the fifth grade, I hated golf, and I didn't own one pair of plaid shorts. That's when I turned to the Sammy house—Sigma Alpha Mu. A like-minded group of fellas whom I immediately related to, with the help of a little upright piano located in their living room. I found my audience. I met a lot of terrific guys who I'm still friends with and a lot of very nice-looking sorority girls who loved to hear me and only me sit and play that piano for hours on end. (*Hey, I can dream, can't I?*)

Of course, before you can become a member of any house, you have to go through a hazing or two of some form or another. I'm sure there were many fraternities who based their existence on the movie *Animal House*, but Sammy? They were pretty light on the crazy stuff. I didn't mind that week of whacked-out events and activities, as I found the whole networking thing to be worth the short period of discomfort, lack of sleep, and embarrassment. (*Hell, hadn't I already been through seventeen years of that at home?*)

Friday

Dear Adam,

I didn't send you to college to brush toilets with a toothbrush. You have to get out of that fraternity and concentrate on your studies!

Love,

Mom

P.S. Toilets are receptacles for disease.

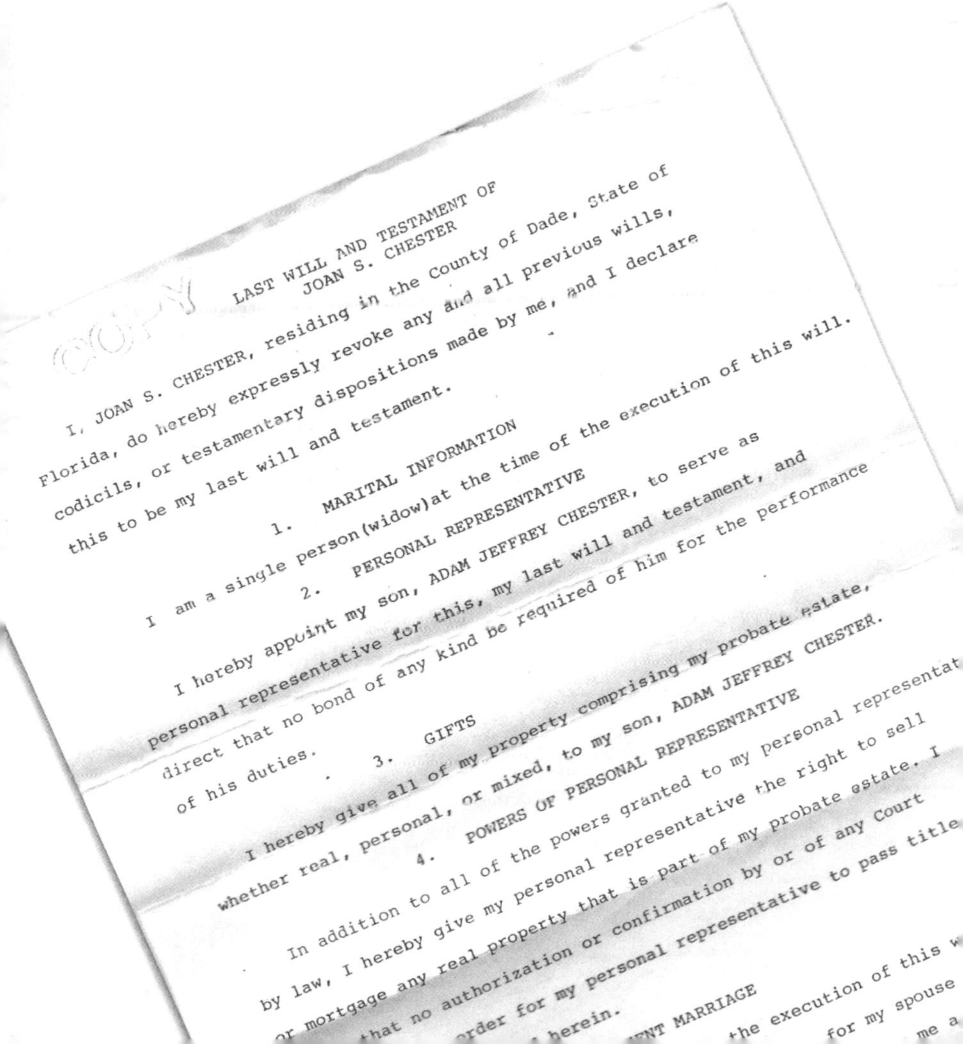
COPY

LAST WILL AND TESTAMENT OF
JOAN S. CHESTER

I, JOAN S. CHESTER, residing in the County of Dade, State of Florida, do hereby expressly revoke any and all previous wills, codicils, or testamentary dispositions made by me, and I declare this to be my last will and testament.

1. MARITAL INFORMATION

I am a single person (widow) at the time of the execution of this will.

2. PERSONAL REPRESENTATIVE

I hereby appoint my son, ADAM JEFFREY CHESTER, to serve as personal representative for this, my last will and testament, and direct that no bond of any kind be required of him for the performance of his duties.

3. GIFTS

I hereby give all of my property comprising my probate estate, whether real, personal, or mixed, to my son, ADAM JEFFREY CHESTER.

4. POWERS OF PERSONAL REPRESENTATIVE

In addition to all of the powers granted to my personal representat by law, I hereby give my personal representative the right to sell or mortgage any real property that is part of my probate estate. I that no authorization or confirmation by or of any Court order for my personal representative to pass title herein.

NT MARRIAGE

the execution of this w for my spouse me a

I don't think I'd ever seen the word "receptacles" used in a sentence. Very interesting. You really *do* learn a lot in college, don't you? And to clarify, a toothbrush never entered the picture. So what if a bunch of the Sammies asked me to reach into a urinal while blindfolded in order to pull out a rotten banana? Big deal. This was all part of life at a university. I just made the untimely mistake of sharing the news with my mother. I also realized that if any of my frat brothers were to have found that letter, I guarantee you the word "toothbrush" would have been my new name.

There were letters that contained far too much information for any eighteen-year-old kid to be told by a parent. Take this one, for example. Here are three things you'll need to know to better understand it: Graham = someone my mother dated. Dundee = someone my mother never dated, but admired. Adam = me = my mother's son = someone who'd have preferred never opening this.

Thursday

Adam—

This guy (Graham) really is a jerk! He's no Dundee either! He's not at all masculine. A wimp! I can't stand weak men! That's why he likes that German lady. She's happy to take control and, Adam, I can't go to bed with someone that turns me off! I don't think you could either!

I don't know if there's anyone out there for me. If not, I'll just do the best I can on my own. I'd rather be alone than put up with someone's behavior that makes me want to throw up. If I weren't so particular, I could have been remarried 10 times already!

Take care of you for me. You're the most important man in my life. (Until another comes along.)

Love,

Mom

Yikes! I don't care WHO my mother is sleeping with. For that matter, just WHO was this guy Graham, and why would he be sleeping with my mother? Scratch that. I don't want to know. It's getting far too Oedipal for me. All I know is that I didn't want to be the most important man in my mother's life. It sounded too weird. And back then, I didn't have time to be the most important man in ANYONE'S life.

My mother decided to sublet an apartment in New York. She felt like she had lived in Miami Beach long enough, and was ready to move. I was happy for her. Happier for me because I knew New York was no closer to California than Miami. I was ready to take on the world. Solo. I decided to audition for a campus production of the musical *Fame*. If you remember the original movie, it featured a character named Bruno who was the piano-playing god; the voice and composer of the show's musical extravaganzas. It was a big role, and I felt like it was made for me. Although I hadn't memorized lines since starring in a fourth-grade production of *My Fair Lady*, this was Hollywood, baby, and I believed I was ready to act. Luckily, after a good audition, I landed the role! Unluckily, the people running the show didn't clear the rights for us to perform *Fame* in its entirety on stage, so the cast could only perform the *music* from the show. Since that would have taken only about twenty minutes, we were asked to choose any other song *not* from *Fame* that we wanted to sing. Without a second thought, I chose my favorite Elton John masterpiece, "Funeral for a Friend." I remember telling my mom, who insisted on flying to LA to see me perform that spring. "Wouldn't miss it," she said. But it was never about the joy of her coming to visit . . .

Wednesday
Adam—
Enclosed find this insurance document in case my plane crashes. Looking forward to seeing you in the show.
Love,
Mom

Yes. The warmth of a mother's love, and the threat of air disaster. And all in two sentences. Like a slice of haiku.

It was more about the possibility of the doom she had to face by visiting me. And to document her bravery on paper, before stepping onto any airplane, she would spend a few minutes and a few dollars purchasing flight insurance to mail me directly from the airport. This would pretty much guarantee me some major money if (*and when*) her plane didn't safely land. Of course, she not only made it safely to the show, but she ended up being a huge hit on campus with practically everyone. They all thought she was the best mom EVER for flying out to my show and hanging with all my new friends (*wherever we went*). But I knew she had an agenda. She was merely tagging along to make sure I was "safe" or to be there in case I, I don't know, needed a sweater? You name it, she was checking it all out. Yet I felt like Chief Inspector Dreyfus from the Pink Panther movies in that I was the ONLY person who recognized what was REALLY going on here. To everyone else, she was Supermom. To me, she was casing the joint.

She met my classmates, some of the parents who were around at the time, and a few of my teachers, including my music theory/composition teacher, Dr. "Skip" Lauridsen. I consider him one of the finest teachers I ever had and one of the most talented classical composers I've ever known. Skip gave me the hardest time because he loved to push his students. No one had really pushed me before Skip. "You can do better than that!" "Try not to be so predictable in that song!" Whatever it was he said, I realized I wasn't the "Anything-I-do-is-simply-splendid" guy that I had been (*and still am*) to my mother. What a wake-up call that was for me. Skip didn't always give me the best grades, but that only made me work harder. He also irritated the hell out of my mother.

Tuesday

Adam—

I don't understand why your music professor is giving you a hard time. Do you want me to talk to him?

Love,
Mom

Oh, sure. Dr. Lauridsen? You remember my mother. She just
wanted a few minutes of your time to discuss changing that C you
gave me to an A. Do you mind? Great.

It was during my sophomore year at school when personal freedom and I took a little vacation from each other. I was riding in the
front passenger seat of a friend's Pinto (*remember those?*) long before seat belts were the in thing (*or required by law*) when his car
was struck head-on by another vehicle. The driver of the other car
was heavily intoxicated and arrested on the spot. Everyone was fine
except for me. I was knocked unconscious and had to be pried out
of the Pinto (*after going half-way through the windshield*) and taken
directly to a local hospital with a fractured hip, an injured eye, and
various bloody cuts and bruises. My mother was contacted, and she
immediately flew out from New York (*with no insurance policy, by the
way*) to be with me. After the surgery to remove a few little bone frag-
ments from my right hip, I soon returned to my dorm on crutches.
Now get this: My mother decided to tag along with me and take up
residence IN the dorm—you know, to make sure I fully recovered.
Four college dudes and my mother. You couldn't make up this kind
of shit. Was it a sitcom? A shitcom? No wait . . . I've just invented a
word . . . it was a sitmom! (*Sitmom* © 2011 *Adam Chester.*)

A couple of my roommates actually got a kick out of my mother's
awkward interactions with all things Adam. This was the round-the-
clock version of my junor high locker room event. My mother was
in our apartment for our breakfasts, our lunches, and our dinners,
and she invaded our space with an energy that no dorm should ever
be forced to know. There were plenty of motels, YMCAs, and bus
benches she could have slept on, but my dorm apartment was perfect. It was free of charge, and I lived in it. I recently took a moment to
speak with one of my roommates from this particular era who we'll
call "Michael" because that's his name. In our phone conversation,

he revealed the following:

"It was surreal. All of a sudden, this woman was there, asserting her role into all of our lives. Mrs. Chester wanted to be everyone's mother. My strongest memory was when she purchased a new outfit. I can still picture it. It was a butterscotch-colored pantsuit. Very rich looking. She was going out on a date." "A date?" I asked him. "A date," he replied. "But I was just out of the hospital. You know, recovering. Who was she going out on dates with?" I asked.

My old roommate continued, "Oh, she went out on several dates and told me EVERYTHING about them. She asked me how she looked in that outfit and modeled it for me." I began to slither down my office chair as I listened to him tell me this. According to Michael, on several occasions she told him the guy she was going out with that particular night was "the guy" she would end up marrying. How weird that must have been for poor ol' Mike, who didn't know her from . . . well, Adam. The thing was, there was NOTHING HE OR ANY OF MY ROOMMATES COULD DO. They just found themselves in the circumstance of her living with us. Michael went on, "It was bizarre, loud, and all consuming—her existence in our apartment revolved solely around you and her. Then, there were YOUR issues of having your mother living with us at college." And that's exactly what she was doing. Could this have been her plan all along?

You might ask where I was during all of this. Painkillers. Lots of them. After a couple of weeks of those, I arose from the *Dating Game* going on outside my bedroom door and headed back to my classes. I was moving to and fro comfortably on crutches, going out on weekends, and hanging out at night with my friends. Only problem was, when I'd come back to my apartment, there SHE was. My mother. And whenever she felt as though everyone was getting tired of having her around, she would go out food shopping for us and/or make us dinner to get back in our good graces. Michael finished our recent phone conversation by telling me that they were all somehow enchanted by her, as she was totally different from any other mother figure they had ever known. "Your mother had some endearing qualities that made her sticking her nose in everyone's business somehow more bearable . . . Mrs. Chester was everybody's friend." Great. Nice talking to you, Michael. Next time you see me, do me a favor? Kill me.

When December vacation finally rolled around that year, my "roomie" and I flew to Miami. I told her she would never again be allowed west of the Mississippi. For a while, that actually worked and she remained back east.

My mother has this ability to strike up a conversation with anyone, anywhere, anytime just to work the word "Adam" into the topic. "Excuse me, sir, but what's that book you're reading? Oh, that's terrific. You know my *son* reads?!" Though even when the dialogue truly concerns my affairs, her judgment isn't always sound, and sometimes the dumb-blonde routine kicks in and she just checks out. All gone. No patience or discipline to get involved with specifics.

Take for example the time she arranged to have my Cutlass driven back to me for my junior year at USC. (*Heaven forbid I should be without my own wheels and suffer the consequences of another car accident.*) She found a company by the name of Dependable Car Travel. Of course she checked them out and did everything to make me feel comfortable about having my beloved car driven back to me across the country by total strangers. Right?

In the letter she sent me to confirm everything, she begins with the words "Dependable," "UCLA prospects," and "phone contacts." Great job, Mom. All good. But then . . . wait . . . what? What about my tapes in the trunk? Fingerprinted? Who? Not from the United States? What does that have to do with . . . ? I don't understand. Who are these . . . ? Mom?

Mooooooooooooooooooooooooooooooooooooooooooooooom!!!!?!

September 9, 1983
Dear Adam,
Your car is leaving today for California. Two guys in their late 20s are going out to look into UCLA for themselves. They're supposed to be in California Saturday the 17th.

Dependable Car Travel has an office in California—
number is XXX-XXXX.

Just get the car from them—(the guys). I gave them
your telephone number out there. Don't get involved
with those guys. They're not citizens of the U.S. They
only have resident cards. They were being fingerprinted
by the agency when I called as they do with anyone who
takes a car.

I hope there were no tapes in the trunk that have not
been copywritten [*sic*].

There's no reason to call the office—but they told me
to give you the number anyhow.

I'll be happy when you finally get your car!

Love,

Mom

I got my car. I got my cassettes. I also got a bicycle, a set of large
power tools, some very cool trading cards, and a new color TV.

And luckily, I (*and I alone*) would have a place to put all that stuff
once I inherited the family fortune, as my mother clarified for me in
this addendum to her last will and testament.

Saturday

September 24, 1983

Dear Adam—

You know my will that you had in your drawer in your
apartment last year—Where did you put it when you
packed up to come here for the summer? It's very
important that you don't lose it—When you find it, make
sure the age in it for you is 18 not over. Because I'm sure
I wrote that after you're 18 yrs. of age, everything I own
goes to you.—You need to have that will if anything, God
forbid, happens to me. So no one can take anything from
you. Please find it and keep it in a good place.

Saturday
Sept. 24, '83

Dear Adam —
You know my will that
you had in your drawer in
your apartment last year —
Where did you put it when
you packed up to come here
for the summer? It's very
important that you don't
lose it — either you find it
make sure the age isn't —
you is 18 not over. Be__
I'm sure I wrote that y__
age is 18 yrs. of age, ever__
I own goes to you. — You a__
to have that will if
thing, God forbid, hap__
to me. So no one can t__
anything from you.

My life insurance policy with Mutual of Omaha for
$20,000 and $10,000 with the State of Florida names
you the beneficiary in all I have but I want to make sure
no one else gets it. And of course, the car which, when I
get the title, I'll turn over to you.

Keep this letter too and don't throw it out 'cause it
also proves my intent. I don't want any good-wishing
relatives to say they will handle the money for you!
You're old enough to handle it yourself and anyhow,
insurance is not considered part of an estate. So the
insurance, in any event, goes right to you! I don't want
Nan or Pop or Michael or Bonnie to get their hands on it!
You're my son and the only one to have it!

Keep this letter in a good place and find the will!
Love,
Mom

Hmm . . . how about I include a picture of your letter in a book
I'll write one day? I digress . . . though I think I finally understand
her point. I'll inherit $30,000 and some car she didn't quite own yet.
Check. Got it. Nan, Pop, Michael, and Bonnie didn't deserve to be a
part of that gravy train.

I felt as though I had been deprived my entire life. I was innocent,
naïve, and pretty much a blank canvas prepared to soak up everything
around me in and out of class. Yet it was the plethora of information
I found in my mother's letters that ended up enlightening me to the
things that truly mattered. Knowledge any proud son would pass on
to future generations. In just a few short words, I learned about . . .

Home Ec and self-esteem:

Wednesday
Dear Adam—
Just a note to remind you that if you have to pay anyone

for anything, write a check from your checking account.
Do not pay any other way. If you don't have enough in
your checking account, wait until you do before you pay
any bills. I have a busy day tomorrow so I'll try to get to
bed early.
Love,
Mom
P.S. You have a beautiful nose! Don't let anyone touch it!

Hope:

Adam—
Encl. find article I found in local paper—I guess there's
hope for me yet!
Love,
Mom

I WISH TO MEET A NICE JEWISH MAN
    About 85 to 100 Years Old. For Steady Company and
Maybe It Will Lead To Marriage.
    I am Alone and Very Lonesome.
    I am a Nice Little Lady, Very Pleasant And Unhappy
Because I Hate to be Alone.
Hopefully Yours
Pauline
My Phone Number is ███-████ in Miami Beach.

Chinese people:

Friday
Dear Adam,
Please take care of the car because even when we

Mom—

Encl. Find Article
I Found in Local
Paper — I Guess
There's Hope For me
yet!

Love,

Mom

**I WISH TO MEET A NICE
JEWISH MAN**
About 85 to 100 Years Old.
For Steady Company and
Maybe It Will Lead To
Marriage.
I am Alone and Very
Lonesome.
I am a Nice Little Lady, Very
Pleasant And Unhappy
Because I Hate to be Alone.
                **Hopefully Yours
                        Pauline**
**My Phone Number Is
532-2566 In Miami Beach.**
ADULT SERVICES

trade it in, it should be in good condition. Take it over
to Marian's mechanic and tell him who sent you. He's
Chinese and he won't rip you off. Get an estimate.
Love,
Mom

Jaywalking:

November 8, 1983
Dear Adam,
Just a note to tell you not to jaywalk. A young girl
walked across the street at night, not at the corner
where a light was, and was hit by a car. Don't jaywalk!!
Love,
Mom
P.S. I know you think I'm crazy, but I don't care!!

The need to do good in life:

I'm so proud of your grades. You really don't have to
get all A's!! I don't know what you're trying to prove!
You're a better man than I, Charlie Brown.

(Golly. Maybe she's not so bad, after all. Except . . .)

Forgiveness:

November 14, 1983
Dear Adam,
I found out the other day that Dr. Weil, when you were

going with Ida, had spoke to Ida's father 'cause they're friends and told him he didn't think it was a good idea for you and Ida to get serious. That's why Ida's father called you in his office! So Leonard was the villain there! Not that it matters now, but you see how all things eventually come out in the wash. Don't bother doing anything now. God is punishing him. They think he has cancer of the throat. Maybe he shouldn't talk so much! In the future when you see him, you could tell him you know.

Love,

Mom

Whoa! I just read that letter for the very first time! I've never heard my mother be so angry at someone who did absolutely nothing to her! Ida was my high school sweetheart in Miami. My first sexual partner. And like most people and their first encounters, you believe you're going to end up together forever and ever and ever.

Dr. Leonard Weil was a friend of our family for decades! I'm pretty sure he never would have said anything to Ida's father about our relationship. Even if he did, I wish I could thank him now for having kept me from doing something stupid at a very young age. Unfortunately, Dr. Weil stopped talking for good many years ago.

Don't get my mother wrong. She doesn't mean anyone any harm, as long as you leave the kiboshing of my love life to her. She can be quite sentimental too! Observe this Valentine's Day card she sent me. So sweet. So normal. Until you hit the word "over" and the true ADAM'S MOM EXPERIENCE begins. This also began the era of "Adam's pet names," or as I liked to call it, "ONE MORE WAY FOR ADAM TO GET THE SHIT KICKED OUT OF HIM IF THIS LETTER WAS TO HAVE BEEN DISCOVERED BY ANYONE AT THE TIME IT WAS RECEIVED." Is it ever OK to be called "Poppy-seed" after the age of five?

...iS HARD TO
FIND!

HAPPY
VALENTINE'S DAY!

Dear,
        I couldn't
have anyone or anything
be much be I love
you. You are very convinced
bi-pointed. — Love
(ever)
        Mom

Don't Go Skiing up
yet — give your leg
a chance to heal —
Don't Trust that
Guy — Gene — that
I've been dating and
no longer are —
keep drying the Reids
I'll keep you informed
of current events —
I love
very happy, Becil —

BOV 25 04

0 74720 00161 6

80VOK356

BUZZA

Adam,

I couldn't love anyone or anything as much as I love you.
You are my constant inspiration.

Love,

Mom

(over)

Don't go skiing yet—Give your hip a chance to rest—
Don't trust that guy—Gene—that I've been dating and
no longer are—Keep drying the dishes—I'll keep you
informed of current events—I love my Poppy-seed—

Again, with the dishes. And who are these MEN she keeps dating?
Obviously there's something wrong with them if she's worried about
what they'll do (*TO ME!*) after she stops dating them.

And the pet names didn't stop with "Poppy-seed" either. Here are
just a few of the other choice nicknames she has for me:

"Picklehead," "Pussy Cat," "Bone Man," and my personal fave,
"Dolly-Poo-Poo." That one made ME feel like kicking the shit out of
me. But she always did her best to fill me with the confidence any
young college student should have when trying new things . . .

Sunday

Adam—

Enclosed find $20. Have lunch on me.

Love,

Mom

P.S. You don't know how to ski! So, if you go to Colorado
skiing, you have to go where beginners are. You don't
want to wear crutches.

Yeah, thanks. You guys have fun. I wouldn't want to get hurt again
so I'll just hang out here in the cabin and watch *The Other Side of the
Mountain*.

As I was putting everything together for this book, I realized it wasn't always *what* my mother was writing about, but what she *wasn't* writing about. For example, let's talk 1984 for a moment. This was the year when two talented USC film schoolmates, Howard and Scott, and I wrote a script to go along with one of my original pop songs appropriately called "Think I'm Goin' Crazy." We were able to solicit the help of everyone in and around USC and proceeded to shoot a music video for a mere $3,500. That included locations, crew, equipment, and editing. After it was finished, I flew to New York and approached MTV, still in its virgin years, with the possibility of having them feature it on their original program *Basement Tapes*. *Basement Tapes* was a video competition show where viewers at home would watch six videos by unknown artists, and then, for fifty cents per call, phone in and vote for their favorite. The artist who received the most calls would ultimately receive a recording contract from a major record company.

Within two weeks after I dropped off the video at their offices, MTV phoned me at my dorm at USC and told me that I was chosen to be one of the six bands featured on a particular episode! That was more than an exciting school day for me; this was the chance of a lifetime.

When the show aired, my video immediately jumped ahead in the polls and stayed that way for most of the broadcast. Then I remember when the host came back on, good ol' VJ Martha Quinn, and announced the winner. "It was *very* close," she exclaimed, "but the winner by *one* percent of the vote is . . ." I took a deep breath. "The Triplets!" Ouch. Our video had lost to this group known as the Triplets by one percent of the vote. ONE! I still believe that our video was the most entertaining of the lot, and to this day it makes me laugh as the extraordinary time capsule of the 1980s it has become. (*What was I thinking wearing that sleeveless T-shirt?*) Anyway, in retrospect, it's not the one percent loss or my sleeveless tee that's so odd. What seems peculiar is this letter I received from my mother just one week or so after my video debut aired on national television:

Tuesday

Adam—

Just a note to say if you buy U.S. Savings Bonds, you
have to keep them in a safe deposit box at the bank so
no one can steal them.

Love,

Mom

Fine. I'll give credit where credit is due. She *was* right about the
bonds...

But when it came to just plain weirdness, my mother was on par
with the master of the macabre, Stephen King. Did you ever read *Misery*? The movie version starred Kathy Bates as the character Annie
Wilkes. I swear if you can read this letter that I received early in my
senior year in the voice of Annie Wilkes, you'd think it was actually
written by her. Do it. I'll wait here.

Tuesday

Dear Adam—

Did you ever get the signal lights fixed on the car?
Also, did you ever get the contact lenses cleaned to
your liking? Otherwise, I have to call the office where I
bought them.

    Did you ever call MasterCard to find out about the
$6.00? I paid them for the car and the additional air
money.

    I have to go now.

Love,

Mom

See? Spooky, huh?

How about a letter on a long piece of blank paper that only says
"Hello—"?

Hello —

Like I'm being stalked!

And she obviously had access to some personal details about my life, including my bank account information, and was somehow able to juxtapose those facts with completely unrelated prose.

Adam—

I don't know if you've been deducting all checks from your bank account! After you put in $1,000, you took out $200 cash. That left $800. $80 for beauty parlor, $150 medical insurance for B'nai B'rith, $150 airline ticket from $800 leaves a balance of $420.

You have a virus. Drink lots of liquids and get plenty of rest and take your medicine. Make sure your bowels are functioning. You get rid of infection by moving your bowels everyday. If you drink enough liquids, they will move.

It's hard to be away when I know you don't feel well. I feel responsible because I probably gave you the germ. I feel helpless since I can't do anything to help from here. Don't worry about William Morris. They only handle well-known people. You'll get someone from a record company to handle you.

Love,

Mom

"I probably gave you the germ"? Just how does one do that from across the country? And notice how she seamlessly weaves between the William Morris Agency and bowel movements. As karma would have it, twenty-seven years after that letter arrived, I signed a contract with William Morris, who helped me secure this book deal. And then the next day, I pooped.

In the spring of 1985, I graduated from USC with a degree in music. It was during that summer when I plunged into therapy and medita tion in order to help me blossom into the independent man I knew I needed to become. HAD to become. Of course my friends back east thought that was a very "California" way of going about it, but I was now officially a Californian. Within days of my first session, I learned how to mantra myself into the next era of my life.

2.

A Boy's Best Friend Is NOT His Mother

I'm a grown man now. I can take care of myself.
I'm a grown man now. I can take care of myself.
I'm a grown man now. I can take care of myself.
I'm a grown man now. I can take care of myself.
I'm a grown man now. I can take care of myself.
I'm a grown man now. I can take care of myself.
I'm a grown man now. I can take care of myself.
I'm a grown man now. I can take care of myself.
I'm a grown man now. I can take care of myself.
I'm a grown man now. I can take care of myself.
I'm a grown man now. I can take care of myself.
I'm a grown man now. I can take care of myself.
I'm a grown man now. I can take care of myself.
I'm a grown man now. I can take care of myself.
I'm a grown man now. I can take care of myself.
I'm a grown man now. I can take care of myself.
I'm a grown man now. I can take care of myself.
I'm a grown man now. I can take care of myself.

I'm a grown man now. I can take care of myself.
I'm a grown man now. I can take care of myself.
I'm a grown man now. I can take care of myself.
I'm a grown man now. I can take care of myself.
I'm a grown man now. I can take care of myself.
I'm a grown man now. I can take care of myself.
I'm a grown man now. I can take care of myself.
I'm a grown man now. I can take care of myself.
I'm a grown man now. I can take care of myself.
I'm a grown man now. I can take care of myself.
I'm a grown man now. I can take care of myself.
I'm a grown man now. I can take care of myself.
I'm a grown man now. I can take care of myself.
I'm a grown man now. I can take care of myself.
I'm a grown man now. I can take care of myself.
I'm a grown man now. I can take care of myself.
I'm a grown man now. I can take care of myself.
I'm a grown man now. I can take care of myself.
I'm a grown man now. I can take care of myself.
I'm a grown man now. I can take care of myself.
I'm a grown man now. I can take care of myself.
I'm a grown man now. I can take care of myself.
I'm a grown man now. I can take care of myself.
I'm a grown man now. I can take care of myself.
I'm a grown man now. I can take care of myself.
I'm a grown man now. I can take care of myself.
I'm a grown man now. I can take care of myself.
I'm a grown man now. I can take care of myself.
I'm a grown man now. I can take care of myself.
I'm a grown man now. I can take care of myself.
I'm a grown man now. I can take care of myself.
I'm a grown man now. I can take care of myself.
I'm a grown man now. I can take care of myself.
I'm a grown man now. I can take care of myself.
I'm a grown man now. I can take care of myself.
I'm a grown man now. I can take care of myself.

I'm a grown man now. I can take care of myself.
I'm a grown man now. I can take care of myself.
I'm a grown man now. I can take care of myself.
I'm a grown man now. I can take care of myself.
I'm a grown man now. I can take care of myself.
I'm a grown man now. I can take care of myself.
I'm a grown man now. I can take care of myself.
I'm a grown man now. I can take care of myself.
I'm a grown man now. I can take care of myself.
I'm a grown man now. I can take care of myself.
I'm a grown man now. I can take care of myself.
I'm a grown man now. I can take care of myself.
I'm a grown man now. I can take care of myself.
I'm a grown man now. I can take care of myself.
I'm a grown man now. I can take care of myself.
I'm a grown man now. I can take care of myself.
I'm a grown man now. I can take care of myself.
I'm a grown man now. I can take care of myself.
I'm a grown man now. I can take care of myself.
I'm a grown man now. I can take care of myself.
I'm a grown man now. I can take care of myself.
I'm a grown man now. I can take care of myself.
I'm a grown man now. I can take care of myself.
I'm a grown man now. I can take care of myself.
I'm a grown man now. I can take care of myself.
I'm a grown man now. I can take care of myself.
I'm a grown man now. I can take care of myself.
I'm a grown man now. I can take care of myself.
I'm a grown man now. I can take care of myself.
I'm a grown man now. I can take care of myself.
I'm a grown man now. I can take care of myself.
I'm a grown man now. I can take care of myself.
I'm a grown man now. I can take care of myself.
I'm a grown man now. I can take care of myself.

Sun.

Adam—

If you go to the beach—make sure you go where there is
a life-guard near—It's much safer if you're going in the
water—

Love,

Mom

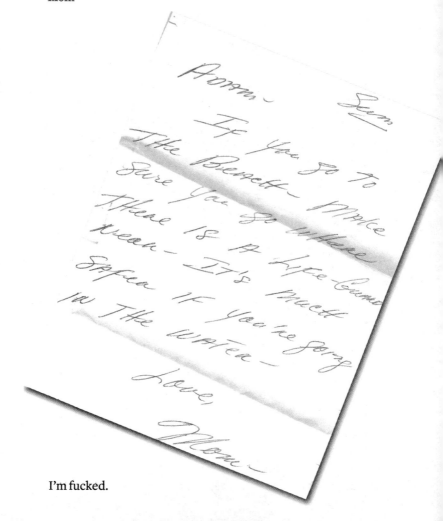

I'm fucked.

Anyway, where was I? Oh, yes. A college graduate.

I had moved into this groovy high-rise two bedroom, two-bath apartment in the Hollywood Hills. My college roommate Tim and I split the larger bedroom, while one of my college girlfriends, Gretchen, scored the other bedroom and bathroom all to herself. (*I still hadn't grasped the idea that in the real world, one could have their OWN room.*) The place screamed "PARTY!" with a view of Hollywood's lights, a humongous balcony to walk out on, plush rented furniture, and a shiny black grand piano I purchased sitting pretty on the Berber carpet. It was the perfect after-college pad, which I managed to keep my mother out of. But that didn't stop her from warning me about the people living in it with me . . .

Thursday
Dear Adam,
I called to say hello and Gretchen told me she has a strep throat! Please don't you catch it as you're coming home soon! Don't drink from her glass or anything like that! Don't forget, you are allergic to penicillin.
Love,
Mom

I got my first job selling records and renting videos at a local music store in the center of the city. It didn't pay much, but I wanted a job that would allow me the time and freedom to pursue my music career, and still play piano at various local restaurants and bars in the evenings. It was in that fall of 1985 when I was introduced to R & B legend Barry White. That's right, THE Barry White! After hearing my music (*which was very R & B at the time*), he expressed an interest in producing me and taking me on the road as his opening act! It was all very exciting, as I'd always been a huge fan of *his* music. He was a big, big man who loved to give big, big bear hugs every time we'd meet to discuss his plans for my future.

Enter Barry White Jr. He was to be the second half of this new act. I was to write all the music and lyrics, play keyboards, and sing, while Barry Jr. would, well, dance. And that was sort of it. Barry Sr. had a vision of Barry Jr. and me becoming the next General Public. (*They were a big black-and-white singing duo in the 1980s.*) Barry Sr. came up with the name Bachet (*pronounced Ba-shay*). It was a synthesis of the "Ba" from Barry and "Chet," in honor of my father's nickname in college. I should have jumped at the opportunity to move forward, but got discouraged by an attorney who told me I'd be a fool to sign the contract Barry Sr. put in front of me—giving him 100 percent of my publishing, forever. Remember, I grew up believing not to trust ANY-ONE, so I passed on the whole thing and Barry Sr. never spoke to me again. I figured I was still young, a college graduate; I had my talent, my wits, and a wad o' cash comin' my way from my mother one day. Life would present me with many other opportunities to blow. I had to have faith.

Speaking of my mother, she never said one word to me about Barry White. Instead, she helped me focus on the more positive, important things. Like becoming a responsible adult, investing money, and building a life for myself while finding a good single woman to share it all with. And that wouldn't be a problem for me! No, sir. As long as that woman was hand-delivered to me by a pimp.

Sunday

Dear Adam,

Don't listen to the advice of <u>anyone</u> when it involves money. Everyone will claim to be an expert on the subject, especially when it's not their money! I'm the only friend you have when it comes to money! Because you're the one I'm interested in, and I have no ulteria [*sic*] motive. So before you do anything in regard to money, <u>talk to me first</u> and you won't go wrong.

People have gotten into a lot of trouble because they
have had bad advice. I'm no expert in the matter, but at
least I know where to go to get an expert opinion.

People have been known to buy phony stocks, make
bad investments. It doesn't matter when you have a lot
of money, but when you're on a counted penny, it makes
a big deal of a difference! !

P.S. Stay away from that girl Brandy. I think she and
her "boyfriend" are operating a "con" game and if she
were to go into your apartment, her "boyfriend" would rip
you off and beat you up along with it. Don't go near her.

It's just so weird that my mother goes off about shit she knows
NOTHING about. "Brandy"? "Con game"? What is she TALKING
about? Brandy was some girl I met at a hamburger place and took out
on one date. And as for finances, to this day, my mother doesn't have
an ounce of savings to her name or one, single, solitary investment. I
love how she says "Talk to me first and you won't go wrong" about finances. Seriously? She knows "where to go to get an expert opinion"?
Where? To Brandy?

The moral of the letter is: DON'T ... TRUST ... ANY ... ONE!

Monday
Dear Adam,
I'm at court waiting for a case to be heard so I thought I'd
drop you a line.

It crossed my mind to tell you to be careful of con men
when you're out trying to get your music heard. They'll
promise you this and that and they're very good at what
they do. They'll even try to get you to give them money
to help "promote" your music. DO NOT BELIEVE THEM.
They are promoting for themselves! Anyone who needs
to use your money to get you promoted is a PHONEY.

If they like you, they will see to it that you are

promoted without you spending a dime. Let them spend
their money. Don't be conned! There are people out there
just looking for suckers.
Love,
Mom
They make a business of it—that's how they make money.

Too bad my mother wasn't there to help all those black rhythm-
and-blues artists in the 1950s.

Sunday
Dear Adam,
Since that check bounced and they deducted $30 or so
from your account, make sure you have enough in the
account so that other checks you write won't bounce. I
know something like that can really foul you up!!
    When I told her (Nan) all she said was, Oh! Just don't
trust any other checks from Nan. They're all full of shit.
P.S. Are you getting my mail? You never seem to answer
any of my questions!
Love,
Mom

I don't understand. Did I really need to have my mother monitor-
ing my finances? Wasn't I a responsible grown-up? If I wrote a check
for something, it was good. And if I got a parking ticket, it got paid.

Friday
Dear Adam,
I am writing to you because I refuse to let you hang up
on me anymore. I can't believe you did that. You must
think it's a joke.
    IT HAPPENED TO YOUR FATHER!
    He didn't pay parking tickets and they said they

would bond out a payment schedule. They never did. And one day, you were 6 years old, it was dinnertime and the police came to arrest him for non-payment of parking tickets. Please, go down and pay your tickets. Don't wait for them to come to you because court costs, etc., add up. Don't let it get to that! Don't ignore it!
Love,
Mom

They actually took my dad to the station? (*Personally, I believe he hired the cops to escort him safely the hell outta there, but then again, I could be wrong.*)

But how did my mother even know I GOT a parking ticket? She must have converted my roommates over to her side. Tim and Gretchen (*the one with the strep throat*). Moles.

Meanwhile, back on the other side of the continent, my mother was settling into sunny Miami Beach. It was all very familiar for her, and she had the comfort of being near her mother and her younger half brother, the dreaded UNCLE MICHAEL. (*Hey, if any of you readers want to try a fun game, go grab a microphone. Plug it in to an amplifier and add a bunch of echo. Then, every time you see the words "UNCLE MICHAEL," say them into the microphone and it will sound really cool. A lot more threatening than he ever was. Thanks.*) My mother and my UNCLE MICHAEL (*see?*) had a volatile relationship from the get-go. However, after I graduated from college, he suddenly became much more of a threat to me. Poor UNCLE MICHAEL. He was a nice enough guy. Never did a thing to hurt me or be anything to me but a fucked-up, disconnected, harmlessly drug-addicted relative.

Anyway, letters from my mother soon arrived alerting me to what to do if and when UNCLE MICHAEL ever appeared at my front door in Los Angeles. Unfortunately, the only thing that never did show up at my front door was UNCLE MICHAEL. So, the warnings had to suffice.

Sunday

Adam—

Do not allow Michael (uncle) to stay in your apartment
at any time!

If he shows up—say your girl-friend is there and
there's no room—

If he calls—say the same thing—

He has no way of knowing. Fore-warned is forearmed!

Remember—he is not one you can trust for 1 minute
& if you value your things—Do not allow him in your
apartment at <u>any</u> time—

Love,

Mom

P.S. Don't hesitate to call the police if he gives you
any trouble!

And this one:

Wednesday

Dear Adam,

I needed a ride to court today so Michael, who has the
car all the time, drove me. It was the first time I had
seen him in a long time.

He's sicker than I thought. I don't believe he's in
touch with reality at all! His thoughts do not run in any
kind of logical manner. He's highly agitated, hostile and
aggressive in his behavior. He's disoriented and I believe
he has all the signs of a skitzofrenic (wrong spelling).

And what's even worse! Nan doesn't even see the
problem or chooses not to. All I know is that Michael
is one to stay far away from because if he becomes
agitated or frustrated in any way, he can become
dangerous. Nan told me he carries a gun on himself

Sunday

Alan —

Do not allow Michael
(uncle) to stay in your apartment at any time!

If he shows up — say
your girl-friend is there and
there's no room —
If he calls — say the
same thing —
He Me — no way of having.
Love warned in before-as-no!

Remember — he is not one you
can trust for 1 minute & if
you value your things — Do
not allow him in your
apartment at any time —

Love,

Mom

P.S. Don't hesitate to call
the police if he gives you
any trouble!

Dear Adam,   Friday

        Enclosed find payment that has to be made to NDSL. Also encl
is a check for $50. to help with it.

        Benny sent me a birthday card. Wasn't that nice?

        Nan had given me the key to her safe-deposit box before she lef
she came back I went to give her the key which was supposed to be i
envelope. I hadn't opened it to look inside when she gave it to me.
turns out, there was nothing inside of the envelope. no key. Michael
probably took it before he left to go out of town.

        Just be advised that he is a thief! Do not allow him in your apa
at any time! Forewarned is forarmed. He probably took out whatever
she had in that safe deposit box.   Nan claims that she probably mispl
the key! Naturally, she defends him. Listen to me....

                                                Love,

                                                Mom

1. Don't drink rain-water.
2. there's a resistant form of
   gonorreha going around — Use
   a condom —

because he went into the jewelry business!! He buys
and sells pieces of jewelry.
>I don't even want to know.

Love,

Mom

Maybe *I* would have wanted to know! I love me a little bling every
now and then. And I love how my mother thinks she can accuse anyone else of not being in touch with reality.

The following letter climaxes with two major points that no letter
from a mother to a son should be without. Inappropriate? Yes. Entertaining? You betcha! Mortifying? You KNOW it. I submit to you, Your
Honor, exhibit number 392,410:

Friday

Dear Adam,

Enclosed find payment that has to be made to NDSL.
Also enclosed is a check for $50. to help with it.
>Benny sent me a birthday card. Wasn't that nice?
>Nan had given me the key to her safe-deposit box
before she left. When she came back I went to give her
the key which was supposed to be in the envelope. I
hadn't opened it to look inside when she gave it to me.
As it turns out, there was nothing inside of the envelope.
no key. Michael probably took it before he left to go out
of town.
>Just be advised that he is a thief! Do not allow him in
your apartment at any time! Forewarned is forearmed.
He probably took out whatever she had in that safe
deposit box. Nan claims that she probably misplaced the
key! Naturally, she defends him. Listen to me. . . .

Love,

Mom

1. Don't drink rain-water.

2. There's a resistant form of gonorrhea going around—
Use a condom—

Gonorrhea, of all things. Can you imagine? "I'm a grown man now,
I can take care of..." Ah, fuck it. My penis hurts just typing this. What
is that burning sensation? Owwwwwwwwwwwwergggggggrrrshhhh-
hhhhhhhhhhhhhhah!

I had to get away. Go someplace where she'd never find me. "I
know," I thought. "I'll go to Mexico!" Back in the 1980s in Tijuana,
the city hosted what was known as the Running of the Bulls ("*La
Pamplonada*"). The event took place in a fenced-off part of the main
street that ran through the city. If you've never heard of it, the ob-
jective was to stay alive while running as close to the really live and
dangerous-looking bulls as possible without getting hurt, maimed,
or killed. Sounded like fun to me. So my friend Gary and I decided to
head for the border one day to give it a whirl. Just so you know, Gary
had already lost one of his legs to cancer at a very young age.

Now, what I'm about to tell you may come across as being passive-aggressive. Was I being passive-aggressive? Yeah. But listen, my
mother was harassing me for so long that subconsciously I felt it was
my turn to take the bull by the horn, if you will.

I remember looking around for a public phone booth on that
street in Mexico, in what was to become one of my last moments of
sanity before the event was to start. There in the distance, not too far
from the bull zone, I ran to make my only phone call on that sunny
afternoon in August of 1986 in a country that was not my own. When
my mother picked up, I believe our conversation went something
like this:

Adam: Hi, Mom!
Adam's Mom: Hi!
Adam: Listen, I just wanted to call you. I'm in Mexico now, near
Tijuana.
Adam's Mom: What? The country?

Adam: Right. Right. Yeah, the country! Anyway, my friend Gary
and I are here together and . . .
Adam's Mom: Gary, your friend from school who lost his leg to
cancer?
Adam: Yes, Gary. The one without the leg. Anyway, well, there's
this event here in town called Running of the Bulls, and Gary and
I are gonna take part in it.
Adam's Mom: Running of the WHAT?
Adam: What? Listen, Mom, I'm losing you. I gotta get going. The
bulls are just about to be set free. I'll talk to you later. Maybe.
Adam's Mom: Adam, what are you . . . ?
(*Click.*)

This letter came to me later that year.

Monday
October 6, 1986
Dear Adam,
I told Nan about the bulls in Mexico. She said she saw
people get maimed that way when she was in Tijuana!
She got so upset and hysterical, she said she would have
called the Border Patrol and I got so angry with her. We
had a fight! Anyhow, I told her you're safe now. She
pictured you being caught by that bull. Just thought I'd
tell you, you can't tell her anything! But in the future,
don't do anything so silly because if you had slipped
and fallen, you could have been run over by those bulls!
And I was so sick that afternoon, not knowing what
happened. Please don't do foolish things like that again.
It isn't funny!
Love,
Mom

Talk about bull, why believe anything my grandmother says? She bounces checks. Remember? Regardless, that letter made it clear that I had found a new hobby. If my mother thought the bulls were foolish, wait until she hears about THIS one! Soon I found that it was her letters that kept me growing, maturing, and attempting to do new things. If it sounded risky, I was ready to try it! I'm talking dicey shit like ...

Onions:

Sunday
Adam—
I didn't speak to you all week and I just wanted to hear your voice. Have a good time next weekend and take your stomach medication with you in case you eat onions again.
Love,
Mom

AND ...

Cheese:

Tuesday
Dear Adam—
Just a note to let you know not to eat any kind of foreign cheese. They have found that some French and Spanish cheese is contaminated. So just eat American cheese.
Also, I know it's been raining there a lot and I want you to be careful. I know how the roads are out there when it rains, so please wear a seatbelt and be careful driving. I hope by this time, you have bought an umbrella.
    I will let you know when I will be arriving. It will be in

a couple of weeks.

Love,

Mom

Like the slogan says, "Great cheese comes from happy *American* cows."

In 1987, I tried my hand at one of the most potentially contaminative cuisines ever: love. I met my first serious girlfriend while I was in Miami for a holiday visit. She was quite beautiful and smart, and she appreciated a good sense of humor. Ironically, she was very close to her mother, who really didn't want her daughter getting involved with a musician who lived 3,000 miles away. Nonetheless, within a few months, Alisa and I were making plans to travel together to France for two whole weeks! Aside from my little escapade running with the horned cattle, this was to be my first major trip outside of the United States. My mother was living alone in a studio apartment in Miami Beach. I remember the day I told her that I was taking Alisa to Paris for a few weeks. You'd think she'd be happy for me jaunting off to a whole new world with someone I could see naked every day! Whoopie! YaHOO! When do we leave? However, my mother reacted a little differently than I'd imagined. I don't have a letter of it or a recording handy, but trust me. It wasn't all that enjoyable. I believe our conversation in her living room went a little something like this:

Adam: I'm taking Alisa to France for a couple of weeks.
Adam's Mom: WHAT? OH, NO YOU'RE NOT. YOU DON'T KNOW ANYONE THERE AND YOU HARDLY EVEN KNOW HER! YOU'RE NOT GOING! YOU HEAR ME?
Adam: Her dad said he'd pay for our hotels!
Adam's Mom: I DON'T CARE. LISTEN... YOU MIGHT AS WELL TAKE A KNIFE AND STAB ME IN THE BACK! JUST KILL ME!

IS THAT WHAT YOU'RE TRYING TO DO? KILL ME? BECAUSE
THAT'S WHAT YOU'RE DOING IF YOU GO TO FRANCE! KILL
ME!
Adam: I'm starving. You want me to go get a pizza?
Adam's Mom: GET OUT! JUST GET OUT OF MY HOUSE!
Adam: Half mushrooms for me, half Xanax for you, right?
Adam's Mom: [*incomprehensible*]
Adam: I'll be back in an hour or so.

Alisa and I went to France and, alas, my mother survived. We had
a glowingly romantic time riding mopeds thru Cannes together and,
yes, even indulging in the occasional foreign cheese! This was living
like I had never lived before. We listened to music with new ears and
took on life with a new purpose. I was pretty certain that she was
"THE GIRL"!

When we returned to the states, Alisa had decided to move to Los
Angeles to be with me. Her father insisted that we not live together
until one day down the road (*if and*) when we were to be married. I
respected that wish as I was not one to argue with the financier of
fine European vacations.

My mother just wanted me to be cautious and, of course, not to
trust Alisa.

Thursday
Dear Adam,
I hope, when you talk to Alisa, you don't confide
everything in her. Specifically, regarding your financial
condition. She doesn't have to know all your personal
business. You don't know if she repeats it to her mother
or not.

In any event, keep certain things to yourself. If you
get married, that's another matter! But, until that
happens, it's better to remain a man of mystery than

one who bears [*sic.*] all. Girls like a little challenge.
Luvu,
Mom

I'm just a regular guy raised by an ordinary middle-class single mother. Her letter made it sound like I shouldn't divulge to Alisa that I'm really an heir to the Rockefeller estate and let's just see if she would fall in love with me for the simple oppressed man I was just *pretending* to be. You're good, Mom. Check. Got it! Though maybe I should have tipped Alisa off about the guy pretending to be my insane uncle back in Miami . . .

Adam,
Another reminder—
    Don't ever let Michael (your uncle) into your
    apartment.
Love,
Mom

Man, THAT guy simply MUST have been evil. What could have happened between the two of them? I asked my mom's sister, Aunt Bonnie (*who grew up with both of them*) to explain. This is what she had to say: "Your mother hated your Uncle Michael because he was Nan's favorite child and only son. When it came to Michael, he could do no wrong." (*Well,* THAT *sounded familiar.*) Aunt Bonnie continued, "Aside from that, I think your mother could be a little bipolar, chemically imbalanced, and partially paranoid schizophrenic . . ."

Now, where was I? Right. Alisa.

It was time to break out of my shared bedroom and get my VERY OWN pad. I needed a place where Alisa could act as if she weren't living with me on a daily basis, in order to please her parents. Gretchen would have to find someone else to pawn off her strep-throat germs on, as I ended up renting a bachelor apartment with room enough for my grand piano (*just so you know, my old upright from college was*

Adam,

Another reminder -

Don't ever let Michael (your uncle) into your apartme

Love,

Mom

stored in a safe place), a nice television, a futon, and me. (*And Alisa. Shhh.*) The place was on a popular street in Los Angeles called Willoughby. If you are a fan of *The Twilight Zone*, you'll recall the episode "A Stop at Willoughby." It was about a man in his twenties or thirties looking for a little escape from his daily, overworked life. He found it in a town of the aforementioned name that ended up being his idea of heaven. That apartment was a little like that for me, and Alisa and I were truly happy there.

Parents, upon hearing that their kid has moved into the big leagues with his own place, might consider sending some sort of a housewarming present or congratulatory note.

Monday
Dear Adam,
Do you think it's a good idea to leave the piano in the lobby of a building you're not in anymore? Personally, I would put it in storage for $100 for 1 month. It may even cost only $50.

There's something new for roaches called Combat. You can buy it at Ralphs. There's no mess and no smell and it works. I got it for my kitchen.

A thought—Alisa is your girlfriend. But until the two of you "tie the knot," I don't think you should confide about very personal matters. Do you? Some things are better kept confidential.
I love you—
Mom

Who am I, Mom? Batman? WTF? What are these "personal matters" I should keep from Alisa? I wish you'd let me in on the secret you hold. Am I really an alien life force who can only be harmed by roaches found on Planet Earth? I'm close, right?

Adam—

Did you ever stop to consider why you always get so angry with me? I'm only interested in the best for you. I'm not your enemy, and lately, you've been treating me as if I am. If I'm not always positive and do not always come up laughing, it's because I've not always had it easy. I don't have a husband to protect me like some women do, and I've learned not to be so trusting. So, don't be so hard on me and so judgmental. I love you. You know that. And if I say things to irritate you, stop to think where I'm coming from. I only want the best for you because you deserve it.

A thought—and please don't get angry at this . . .

Until you're ready to get married, you should use some protection because you don't want to be a father before any marriage takes place.

Love,

Mom

I wasn't ready to get married. In 1989, Alisa and I broke up. Not soon after, she married an attorney. (*I had a FEELING she was just after my money.*) Anyway, I kept that apartment on Willoughby with my steady flow of income from playing piano five nights a week at a local restaurant. During the day, I learned how to be a travel agent, and eventually got a full-time job booking and ticketing travel for large corporations. It was a high-stress office environment, but it afforded me the luxury to travel first class for little money to faraway places. *Very* faraway places. Very faraway places that were very far away from my mother, who never seemed very far enough away from me.

Speaking of my mother, she soon found Miami to be too hot, too humid, and too close to UNCLE MICHAEL. It was time for her to make a move again. Where could she go? Where would she go? I wasn't sure, but I had an inkling that it'd be a wise move for me to start building a shelter. Changing my identity. Signing up for the government's Witness Protection Program. Anything. Because something was coming. And no one was safe. Not even nuns.

November 7, 1989
Adam,
Just some things you should know about.
    1. In the orange bag in your apartment, there should be my will in there. If not, Leonard Cooperman, in Miami, has the original.
    2. My life insurance is with Mutual of Omaha.
    3. You are not responsible for any of my debts.
    4. Mariah is paid up. The rent was paid either to her, Mariah Bumble, or to her daughter who's a nun in Oakland, CA. It was always paid by check. If she says that some rent is owed because in the past she tried to collect the rent twice from me saying she forgot, just tell her you'll sue her daughter's order in Oakland, for collecting money and not reporting it. That will scare her. She's very protective of her daughter, the Nun. She doesn't want any bad publicity. I'm just telling you this because she, Mariah, is not to be trusted, and I don't want her conning you in any way. Not that I expect anything to happen to me, but, I would want you to know how to handle some difficult issues. And she would try to benefit from the situation especially if she thought you didn't know to whom I paid the rent. The nun's name is Bridget Bumble. Don't let her take advantage of anything.
    Keep this paper so you can refer to some of the names, if you need to. Don't let this letter upset you. I'm just being very methodical. I don't intend to let anything happen to me until I see all of my grandchildren.

Love,
Mom

How can anyone so methodical be so chaotic? So many details about shit. Leonard. Mariah. A nun in Oakland. I don't know who ANY of these people are, nor did I need to know. I just wanted to live my life. Was I being selfish? *Shellfish?*

Sat.
Adam—
Do me a favor—
    Please don't eat sushi!
    Thank-you—
Love,
Mom

At that moment, eating sushi became one of the defining actions of my adult independence: I would eat what I wanted to eat when I wanted to eat it! Yes . . . the worm had turned!

The hour had finally come to shift my gaze somewhere beyond the sea. Perhaps somewhere, waiting for me, was the next contestant in the HOW-LONG-CAN-YOU-DATE-A-GUY-WITH-AN-INSANE-MOTHER SHOW! (*Especially now that the mother would be moving to the same fucking city as her poor fuck of a son.*) Focus.

Enter Dana. She holds the proud distinction of being the first person I ever dated who KNEW I might have a problem with more than just my car tires.

Wednesday
Dear Adam—
That tire has me concerned. You said that your tire was flat and you had it fixed. Well, I don't know how they fixed it, but you can't ride around on a tire that has been patched up. That would be ok for a spare, but not for

SAT.

ADAM —

DO ME A FAVOR —

Please DON'T eat SuSHi !

THANK-you —

Love,
Mom

Worm in sushi startles surgeons

BOSTON — Doctors removing a college student's appendix were surprised when the real cause of his pain wriggled into view: a two-inch-long red worm he had eaten with his homemade sushi.

When the patient came to the hospital in pain, doctors assumed he had appendicitis. But his appendix looked normal during surgery, and as they were about to sew him up, the worm slithered out of his abdominal cavity and onto the surgical drapes.

After he awoke, the man remembered eating raw fish the night before at a friend's home in New York.

Experts say most cases of worm infection in raw fish occur when people prepare it at home.

The case of the 24-year-old student was described in today's New England Journal of Medicine.

everyday use. It's like putting a band-aid on a cut. That
won't heal the cut.

Please go buy a new tire or as many tires as you
need. You can put it on your credit card. You've had the
car for some time now and I'm sure it needs tires. It's
nothing to fool around with, Adam. If the tires are not
good, it's too dangerous. Especially on the highway!

Love,

Mom

Did Dana know what peril lurked ahead? Perhaps. She certainly
witnessed the growing collection of letters I was keeping. "Hey . . .
why are you saving all those letters from your mother? That's a bit
odd, isn't it?" Dana was studying to be a therapist. I'm sure she could
have written her thesis on me. She suggested that I not even look at
the letters. "Just throw them out. They're invasive! Why read them if
they make you sick?"

And now, a phone conversation that likely took place later that
same week:

"Hey, Mom! I met this really nice girl the other day. She's a friend
of an old college friend of mine. She's going to be a psychologist! I
know. Pretty serious! Anyway, she had some advice for me. Yeah.
She thinks I should stop reading the letters you send me all the time.
Yeah. Really."

Thursday

Adam—

My coworker that spoke to you on the phone has a
27-year-old son who just got back with his girlfriend
and he said he told his son to "wrap it up" for at least
6 months and then go for an AIDS test as it takes that
long for anything to show! (Both go.)

He said it's best for any man to keep it wrapped. As it
only takes 1 time!

Play it safe!
Mom

Well, she had a point, but so much for being happy for me. I also wondered what her obsession was with venereal diseases. Didn't she know I had a good head on my shoulders? I decided to call a trusted cousin to see if she could offer some insight to this situation. My cousin Laurie in Las Vegas had known me for many, many years and was quite familiar with my mother's paranoia and general approach to day-to-day living. I asked her why she thought my mother was obsessed with VD. After a long pause on the phone, Laurie replied, "I have no idea. Maybe she loves you?"

"Do you love me, Laurie?" I asked. "Of course I do, sweetie!" Laurie replied. I continued, "Then why haven't you ever written me about venereal disease?"

Dana and I soon found an apartment and moved in together. This was the first time I was to be officially living with a girlfriend around the clock, without having to keep it a secret from the girl's family. And that sounded like the PERFECT reason for my mother to celebrate by moving to Los Angeles.

I started working as a full-time travel agent in a much nicer office, while playing piano a few nights a week. In my spare time, I was pursuing my career as a singer/songwriter by recording my original music in various studios. A friend of mine in the television world was able to place a few of my songs in his made-for-TV movies. Of course, there was NEVER any mention of ANY of that trivial crap (*my dreams, love life, career*) when it came to my mother's correspondence or interactions. She was far too concerned with the goddamn will.

Tuesday
August 21, 1990
Adam—
It's very important that you do not lose the Will. The
Last Will I made named you executor and that's the way

I want it. I had a Will made before with Nan as executor,
and I forgot the attorney's name that has the current
Will but he's in Miami and he worked at the Juvenile
Court House when I was a social worker. He is <u>not</u>
related in any way.

I made this Last Will <u>after</u> I made the one with Harvey.

Please do not lose this letter until you find the Will
because this can be a legal document that a Will does
exist naming <u>you the executor</u>.

Love,

Mom

Joan

Unbelievable! So die already, will ya! Or stop talking about it. A
few months later...

November 7, 1990

Dear Adam—

Just a note to let you know my Will is in that orange
bag that you put away. It is the last one I made and it
has YOU as executor. I made one before that has Nan as
executor. But that was when you were in High School. I
can't remember the attorney's name that made it up for
me in Miami. He was one of the attorneys that I worked
with at Juvenile Court when I was a social worker for
the State. Not that I anticipate anything happening to
me. I just want you to be aware of the facts. All I have is
a life insurance policy with Mutual of Omaha.

Love,

Mom

Enclosed find a picture of the intestines found in a
health food store. Just follow doctor's orders and you'll
be fine.

fined foods and animal products, feces will begin to adhere to the Colon wall resulting in putrefaction and fermentation. This condition will create pathogenic bacteria (fungus) which, when absorbed into the blood system, creates a condition of blood toxemia. This leads to bodily dysfunctions, premature aging and ultimately - cellular degeneration.

Because of the density of the fecal matter clinging to the colon wall, muscular contractions or peristaltic waves are not able to move the hardened feces along the colon, thus creating a condition of chronic constipation.

) creating spastic colon

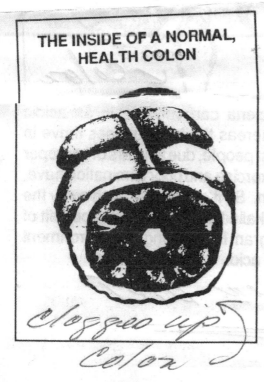

THE INSIDE OF A NORMAL, HEALTH COLON

clogged up colon

...lon, there may be only a narow, tiny opening in the center of the colon. Digested food will have a very hard time going through the colon. In many cases the food and mucus can become impacted and stay in the colon for months and even years.

OF COURSE I had stomach problems. All this talk about death was making me ill. Suddenly I was lactose intolerant. Scratch that. I was EVERYTHING intolerant. It seemed as though anything I ate gave me a stomachache. Fortunately, I had that picture of the intestines my mother sent. I took it with me to each and every doctor I visited back then. They all instantly understood my trouble without my even mentioning her weekend visits to our apartment, her excessive phone messages asking where we were at any given minute, and the letters she continued to send that I insisted on compiling. Now I get it. (*Sorry, Dana.*)

In April of 1992, the LA riots happened. Now everyone in Southern California thought they were going to die. My mother could have started a new club. Instead, she was able to pull some strings and get a job at USC, my old school. This allowed her the chance to relive my life with a fuller and better understanding. She began working as a housemother for a sorority on campus. (*Hey, if you can't be an overbearing mother to ONE, why not be an overbearing mother for ONE HUNDRED and get paid for it?*) Anyway, when the riots actually began, my mother headed straight from the sorority house to our apartment for refuge. She ended up sleeping on our living room couch until the threat of imminent danger subsided.

Let me just say the riots weren't half the terror of her camping out at our place. I don't remember how Dana and I made it through, but I'm pretty sure my mother never received another sleepover invitation. I received this after she went back home to my alma mater . . .

Tuesday

Adam,

I know you and Dana will probably get married some day and I'm happy for you. But I hope you're both being cautious about having children, because you first have to be in a financial position to support them. But I'm sure you and Dana are bright enough to be responsible and then again, it's none of my business.

Love,
Mom

Hmm . . . from the tone of that letter, maybe there was hope for her yet.

Months later, I arranged a trip for Dana and me to head back to Philadelphia to attend my best friend Dave's wedding. At the same time, I planned to reunite with my evil relatives in New Jersey. My uncle Bill (*my dad's brother*), his wife, and my three first cousins decided to meet at a local restaurant in the city. When the day arrived, we all hugged, shook hands, and eventually sat down at a very long table to stare at the piles of pictures Uncle Bill had brought that showed my father at various stages of his life. We brushed up on our family history and shared some of our personal stories, and about three hours later, I was still alive. They hadn't murdered me. I had no idea why I was ever included in their twenty-year feud with my mother. But in the end, just meeting them was a giant step for Adam-kind.

Wednesday
Dear Adam—
Please don't tell Bill or any of his children anything about me. I don't want them knowing anything. It's none of their business. I don't trust them. I had good reason to keep you away for as long as I did. They wanted nothing to do with you or I from the day your father died and they are nothing like you or your father! If you insist on communicating with them, please be careful.
Mom

Rule number one was now null and void. I was convinced that my father's side of the family were not descendants of the Hatfields. On the other hand, my mother was driving a wedge between Dana and me, as the topic of my mother became all we ever spoke about. And my mother's intrusions were endless.

September 3, 1992

Adam—

If your manager does not fix the stove in a short period of time, I will have this lawyer I know write a letter to the owner telling him of the problem. So let me know if you need a lawyer's letter. By law, you have to have a safe operating stove, and if he takes too much time fixing it, the manager is NOT doing his job! Your rent includes a stove and it poses a hazard (safety).

Love,

Mom

P.S. Good luck! And let me know if you need a letter.

I'm afraid of my ex-boss. The one I had the hearing with.

Don't give your address to anyone. She may want to retaliate! (She's crazy.) Also, when you use bomb in the house, you have to rinse dishes and put food away!

(I know, I know. Stop acting like a Mom!)

Mom

It was at that point that Dana and I stopped acting like a couple and decided to go our separate ways. The whole ménage à Mom was too much for her. Dana struggled with it for a long time, as we truly cared for each other. But it was impossible for my mother to just let us be. And believe it or not, I didn't see it. The only thing I saw was that Dana and my mother were constantly pulling me in opposite directions. That must have been exactly the way my father felt with his family and *his* wife. I needed to be alone for a while. I moved into a one-bedroom apartment by myself and began to figure things out.

Perhaps I had been an accomplice to this never-ending drama the whole time? The moment had come (*again*) to ask my mother to leave LA. She, too, understood that the space would do us both some good. She ended up moving back to Miami (*again*) and getting a job as a hostess in a popular deli.

Before she got on the plane, however, she did manage to share a little last-minute career advice, for old time's sake . . .

May 1993

Adam—

Phillip said to send a tape to Darbra Streisand, Malibu, CA, and the postman will deliver it to her as he has her address. You have nothing to lose. Why not try it?

Love,

Mom

OK. Call me a skeptic, but I'm not really sure Barbra Streisand opens her own mail. I guess my mother's male-pal-of-the-hour, "Philip," knew better. After all, he DID know where she lived! (*Please forgive me in advance, Babs, for divulging your whereabouts to the world.*)

As for my mother's move back to Miami, I had faith that she would ultimately find happiness there.

November 24, 1993

Adam—

After I spoke to you today and you asked me if "I was happy," I wondered if something was wrong with you! How could you ask me that? Do you think I've been having a good time?

I have no home, no job, and I'm struggling just to keep a roof over me and you ask "if I'm happy"!!

I haven't seen you in 4 months. I'm lonely and yet you ask me that. Don't you realize what I'm going through?

Nan & Michael are fucking out of their heads and I have no one to talk to. You wanted me out of LA. I should ask, "Are you happy?"

You got what you wanted.

Mom

Whoops.

Well, don't worry . . . my mother wasn't homeless. She was safe in Miami around her mother and her beloved brother. The real issue here was that *I* was happy and that I was successful in basically deporting her (*for now*) from the entire western coast of the United States. Her letter ALMOST made me feel guilty about the whole thing. Then I got this and I immediately felt better.

Adam—

Hopefully—I can see you before you leave for New York
'cause I have something for you that you can use in N.Y.

I hope if ever you have intruders in your apt. while
you are asleep & wake up—you let them have whatever
they want and that way—they won't bother you & leave
you alone. Don't start fighting with them. Keep your
windows locked. You're right on an alley on the 1st floor!

Also—drink bottled water—the pipes in your bldg. are
old & the water could contain lead.

Love,

Mom

(That's how mom's are.)

That just slays me. Is that truly how moms are? Anybody?

About eight months later, when I still didn't have a proper answer to that question, Dana and I decided to get back together. It was easy to fall back in love. It was familiar, it was romantic, and—in the beginning—it was nice again. I wrote my mother a letter to tell her about it, but it came back to me unopened, as I had addressed it to:

Adam's Mom
Miami Beach, FL

I assumed the mail carrier would know her address. Or did I? Hmm . . . do you think I was being passive-aggressive to my mother?

Adam—

Hopefully — I can see you before you leave for New York 'cause I have something for you that you can use in N.Y.

I hope if ever you have intruders in your apt. while you are asleep & wake to — you let them have whatever they want and that way — they won't bother you & leave you alone. Don't start fighting with them. Keep your windows locked. You're right on an alley on the 1st floor!

Also — drink bottled water — the pipes in your bldg. are old & the water could contain lead. (That's how Mom's are)

Love,
Mom

To myself? To the mail carrier?

Anyway, my reunion with Dana was highly charged and everything seemed on course for our relationship to move into marriage. We decided to take a trip to Australia for a little vacation, and since I was a travel agent, it would be first class all the way. Looking back, I'm sure she believed I was going to pop the big question while we were traveling, but I wasn't ready for that. I was too busy worrying about more important things.

> Saturday
> Adam—
> Nan told me to tell you there are sharks in the water in
> Australia. So don't go in the water.
> Love,
> Mom

There she goes again, blaming my grandmother. (*Her mother.*) I recently asked my now-ninety-four-year-old grandmother about this. She didn't remember ever saying that to my mother. Granted, she hardly remembers my MOTHER at this point, but IF SHE DID, I guarantee you she'd have no recollection of ever even saying the word "shark" in a sentence, let alone of giving that advice to me via my mother.

My mother's fear was written all over her face. Every moment of every day was consumed with thoughts over what could possibly go wrong for me, especially while I was out of her reach. Far away. Overseas. She even went to the trouble of having some dude named Larry draw a sketch of her on a napkin that she kindly included in the following letter.

> Sunday
> Adam—
> Enclosed find sketch Larry did of me—don't my eyes
> look sad?

Mom —   Sunday

Enclosed is a sketch I drew
Do of me — Don't my
eyes look sad?

Anyhow Bon Voyage and
have fun —

                    Love,
                         Mom

P.S. Is this a Better note?

Anyhow—bon voyage and have fun—

Love,

Mom

P.S. Is this a better note?

Doesn't that just scream "HAVE FUN—DON'T WORRY ABOUT LITTLE MISS SAD EYES OVER HERE!"? Ah, thank you, Larry (*whoever you are*), for capturing the essence of confidence, joy, and complete lack of fear that was, is, and always will be my mother. (*Are you available for parties?*)

Of course, no going-away present would be complete without a listing of my mother's insurance policies.

NYCERS

New York City Employee's Retirement Services

Just want you to know if anything happens to me, this is the place you call as you are listed as my beneficiary in the event of my demise and you continue to collect $200 a month.

Mom

(over)

Did you know I was the only one in the history of New York City that ever placed 100% on the civil service exam for social workers? I have the letter they sent me to that effect. Nan saw the letter.

To paraphrase: "In the event something does happen to me while you're away having fun in some other part of the world, you'll be well cared for *thanks to me* and you can tell your children (*that you'll eventually have*) that I was the only person to score 100% on a civil service test in New York. And you get $200 a month! Have a great trip!"

When Dana and I returned to California without an engagement ring, it should have been all over. Yet we were caught up in the rou-

tine and decided to move into a condo together in a nice neighborhood, about an hour away from the travel agency I worked for. Word
on the street was that no matter where we fled, there were bad people waiting there for us.

Dear Adam & Dana—
Am at my desk and thought I'd drop a line re: Halloween.
    When you open the door to give out candy, please
make sure it's children at the door as they're having
robbers go out on Halloween to rob people's houses. I
read it in the paper.
    Also, when you go to Miami on Thanksgiving, please
don't give Michael a ride anywhere as he goes to "bad"
places and don't let him drive the car. Just stay far
away from him. Really!! I sent Nan the pictures of you
and me, Adam, in Boston that you gave me.
    Take care of each other.
Love,
Mom

In 1995, my mother had had enough of Miami for good. (*Again.*)
It was time for her to move on with her life. She hopped a flight from
Miami Beach and landed in New York City. (*Again.*) Only THIS time,
my little Jewish mother had a plan.

Saturday
Adam—
This is my plan. When I get the ticket from you to go to
California on Thanksgiving, I'll stay with you for that
weekend. Then, I'll stay with Reva for three weeks. The
lady near Melrose.
    Then, I'll fly to NY on December 26th, stay with Bonnie

for 2 weeks, then move into the woman's residence in NY
and live there while I work at that paper on Wall Street.
I can't stay here any longer than Thanksgiving!!! I'd
rather be dead. This is no place for a nice girl like me! So,
when I call to make my ticket, it will only be 1-way.
Love,
From
Your Lutheran Mom

Bam! The Lord works in mysterious ways.

When I asked her what she meant by her sudden conversion to
the Lutheran faith, she told me that she had just been to a Lutheran
service that week, and was "very impressed with the whole thing."
Ultimately, her newfound religion was still not enough to pardon her
sister, Bonnie, or her nephews, Andrew and Steven.

Friday
Adam—
Nan is leaving next Thursday. I'm going to sleep over
Tuesday night so I can see her for a while.

Bonnie still smokes pot. When she goes to Andrew's
I think they smoke it together. If you're still going over
Christmas vacation to New York, be aware of this. Can
you believe, a father smoking pot?!! Anyhow, call me old-
fashioned or what, but make sure you wear your seatbelt
when you drive with Andrew OR Steve—He smokes too.

If I sleep over at Bonnie's, she stays up late and the
smoke from the pot fills the room. It's not even an "in"
thing to do anymore.

I have sooo much to do when I go to LA. I have to
see Jane, I want to get a tan, get my nails done, and
go shopping at the Beverly Center. And I can't wait to
see you. I haven't seen you in 7 months. Isn't that long
enough?

Much love—
Mom

I wonder if her aversion to pot smoke was part of her Lutheran phase. And do Lutherans like to get tans? And come to think of it, if she likes getting tan so much, why the hell did she move out of Miami?

Friday
Adam—
This is the amount I told you for your birthday. It now comes to the $100. I told you. I bought you a warm hat for the snow. Should I mail it? It's snowing today. I have a cold.
Mom

Once again, let's give it up for Miss Annie Wilkes. Miss Annie Wilkes, everybody!

When it came to sending inappropriate correspondence, my mother apparently had a mailing list of recipients aside from me. Yes, there were others who knew my mother to be "Postal Mom." (Postal Mom © 2011 Adam Chester.) Sadly, I don't believe those people ever responded to her mail either. Even more sadly, some of the other people to whom my mother wrote were the very people I worked with. That's right. You heard me. My mother wrote to my co-workers. And why not?! She believed that anyone, anywhere, who was in any position to have contact with me should be her pen pal.

The travel agency I worked for was a small but busy corporate office that handled the business for many large advertising agencies in the LA area. The staff of this 850-square-foot room consisted of me, one other agent, the owner of the company (*who also booked travel*), and Bill, the gentleman who opened the mail and put together all the tickets for the customers.

Check out these postcards she addressed to the STAFF of Travelcare. I recite the lyrics to the song "You've Got a Friend" whenever

I read these, only it's my mother, not James Taylor singing the lead.
"You just call out my name . . . and you know wherever I am . . . I'll
come running." Sounds pretty. But then I realize she's singing it to
the entire staff of Travelcare. And they are all doomed.

> #1.
> Hi!!
> Here I am in NYC now!
> Love to all—
> Joan Chester
> 6 Charles St.—1D
> N.Y., N.Y. 10014

> #2.
> Hello again from New York! The heat wave broke at last!
> Love,
> Joan

What mother corresponds with people she doesn't really know?
And we're not talking about a holiday card here! Notice the word
"again" in her second postcard. I'm telling you, she wrote to these
poor people all the time just to make sure they knew how to contact her IF (*and when*) anything were to happen to me. (*Again.*) I can
still hear Bill from the office saying "Oh, good . . . it's another postcard from your mom." Seriously, can you say "two-weeks' notice"?
But who could get mad at a mother who was getting on in years and
might croak at any given moment . . .

> Sunday
> Dear Adam—
> As I'm getting on in years, you should know that my
> will is in the piano bench and my life insurance is with
> Mutual of Omaha.
>   There, I feel better.

Old Glory

STER
es ST. ID
N.Y. 10014

Y LOPEZ © CARD #1

REAL PEOPLE P
343 East 5th Street, Brook

Greetings from New York City

1656

Central Park, New York City.
Photo: Atsushi Tomioka

Hello Agnize
From New
York! The Heat
wave Broke at
Last! Love,
Joan

Staff of

PRINTED IN THAILAND

Love,
Mom

Yeah, yeah. $30K and a car she no longer owned. I know, I know.
Though what I want to know is: Who the hell moved the will out of
the orange bag??

Have you noticed a pattern here? Do something embarrassing,
then send a will or an "I'll Be Dead Soon" letter. Those postcards to
my work finally got ME to respond in writing. It's too bad my mother
hasn't been saving MY letters. I mean, letter. From the sound of her
response below, I bet it was a doozy.

Thursday

Adam—

Thanks for the letter. I just realized how unfair I've
been to you. Yes, I have looked toward you as the parent.
(See what happens, roles get reversed). I don't mean
to swamp you with my problems. I'm so thankful you
have someone like Dana that can be there for you and
understands. You're lucky. Hopefully, things will work
out. I love you and you've <u>always</u> been the best son
anyone could have. I <u>do</u> realize I can't be the center of
your life. If I said anything to the contrary, I was being a
spoiled little girl. Ignore it.

Love,

Mom

Thanks for that, Mom. (*I mean, my little girl . . .*)

It was right around then that Dana and I split up for good. Uncer-
tain as to where to go, I moved temporarily into my friend Tim (*one
of the moles from my old apartment*) and his wife's house, while I went

looking for a new place. Turned out to be the most prolific time in my life for writing music. I was off to the recording studio to work on what would be my very first commercial release. I was doing alright, but it was hard at first being without Dana. We had been on and off as a couple for years, though for years we both knew it wasn't working.

> Thursday
> Adam—
> You need to speak to someone. You can do it on a
> Saturday. I'll ask my doctor if he knows anyone in
> LA. Or, you can ask your internist for the name of a
> psychologist. Even your eye doctor (who you like) could
> recommend someone.
>   It's hard when something ends. But, there's always
> a new beginning down the line. Hold your ground. You
> deserve the best and you will get it! You need a help
> mate. Someone that gives, not takes!
> Love,
> Mom
> P.S. Make sure you use rubbers! Don't take chances.

I NEED TO SPEAK TO SOMEONE? Unbelievable. And as for the rubbers, I think my mother missed her calling. She should have looked into getting a job working for the CDC.

I remember the day I first opened this next letter. It was late and I'd just arrived home from a long writing session with a lyricist I'd been working with . . .

> Saturday
> Adam—
> Have you written anything lately?
>   Get Heiden's [sic] classical pieces and listen. There's

many passages you can translate into pop music.
It would be very interesting.
Get busy.
You've let your writing go.
Love,
Mom

Adam slowly looks up from inside the recording studio and . . .
and . . . Scene.

Several months later, I adopted a dog I named Hadgi, and started
seeing a twenty-year-old Armenian girl (*she looked a lot older*) by
the name of Vicky, whom my mother met during a quick visit to LA.
Vicky was young and innocent, and she had no idea how messed up
I truly was.

Adam—
It was a delight seeing you and Vicky. Let me know when
your travel plans materialize so I know what's happening.
Is your car insured for other people to drive?
Love,
Mom

As you can tell, my mother had nothing but nice things to say
about Vicky.

In the fall of 1996, I finished my CD that I appropriately titled
"You Don't Know Me . . . from Adam," and dedicated it to Vicky.
Since I didn't have a major record label deal, my efforts were fo-
cused on getting it distributed to the masses. It would take some

serious grassroots marketing to get the word out about its release. I knew if there was one person who could assist, it was my mother. Obviously, I was right.

> Adam—
> I told everyone at work about the CD. They are all going to buy it! About 20 people!
> Love,
> Mom

A year later, I cashed in on those royalties and took Vicky on a first-class trip to Spain and Morocco.

> May 16, 1997
> Adam—
> Enclosed find a little check to buy brunch for you and Vicky.
> I love you.
> When are you going on your vacation? And where are you going? Are you still going to Spain? Morocco is in South Africa and is nowhere near Spain!
> I'll speak to you next week.
> Love,
> Mom

Obviously, my mother would not be my first choice for the "phone-a-friend" portion of any game show.

When it came to wealth, my mother's strategy always involved things that could instantly change your life. There was never a real plan or a willingness to start on the ground floor and work her way up.

Oh, no. It was always about a gift from someone or a friend helping out, or winning the lottery or coming into possession of a valuable object. Take this letter, for instance.

It's a quarter. Better yet, it's a dirty American quarter from 1994.
Any questions?

This is just a prime example of one of several letters I received
without a single written word on it. But there in the center of the
blank page would be one little item attached with a piece of Scotch
tape. I refer to these as my "I-can-help-you-get-rich-quick-by-tap-
ing-something-to-a-piece-of-paper-that-could-be-worth-a-lot-of-
money-because-it-looks-important-to-me-but-I-can't-really-tell-
you-why" letters. Some displayed pennies. One featured a mysterious key. And this . . . a dirty American quarter from 1994.

Turned out that coin wasn't worth anything more than twenty-
five cents, and the vintage was all wrong. The year I was looking for
was 1998. That was the year I found what money can't buy in the form
of the girl who would soon become my wife and the mother of my
two beautiful children.

3.
He Just Met a Girl Named Maria

It was back in 1992 at an LA club called Luna Park. My percussionist, Theo, and I were playing a set of my original songs for about seventy-five people. An old friend of mine whom we'll call "Zane" went to the show with one of her friends from college. After the show, Zane briefly introduced us. "Adam, Maria. Maria, Adam." The next day, she called and told me that Maria was looking for a piano player to record a song she needed for an upcoming audition. She was an actress. Cool. I got all excited. "Calm down" I remember Zane saying. "You have a girl-friend and she has a boyfriend." Of course I agreed that this would be strictly professional. So what if Maria was stunningly beautiful?

She came over to my apartment one night and I taped the song "Another Suitcase in Another Hall" for her. After a few inspiring moments together, she took her cassette and she was gone. End of story.

Cut to 1998. Six years later. My friend Zane was throwing a little Memorial Day weekend get-together at her place. Vicky and I had just broken up and I wasn't really going out much, but decided to go to Zane's party by myself just to get out for a little bit. As I walked in, I immediately recognized her face. Zane immediately reintroduced us. "Adam, Maria. Maria, Adam. You remember, the piano player?" she asked. From that moment on, Maria and I spent the evening glued to each other, finding out about what each of us had been doing with our lives over the past six years. Maria was now boyfriend-free, still stunningly beautiful, and she knew nothing about my mother. That to me spelled big-time potential. The very next day, we both called Zane to inquire further about each other, and soon set out on our first of many dates. (*I took her to my favorite sushi place.*)

My mother was still living in New York. After a month or so, I decided to give her a call and tell her about this amazing new girl that I was dating, Maria. It was one of those surreal phone conversations that go in a completely different direction than I originally expect. Here is her formal response that arrived days later:

Sunday

Dear Adam,

I heard on National TV that there is a telephone scam on. Con men call on the phone and try to sell you all kinds of things. Get your credit card number and con people. Hang up on anyone on the phone that tells you of a great deal. Someone called me the other day and I hung up on him. He called me back and I told him if he bothered me again, I would report him to the Better Business Bureau. So, be careful of telephone salesmen.

I guess she really didn't hear a word I said to her. I realized there was so much potential here for future warning letters that I didn't want to confess it was I who'd phoned and that we must have had a bad connection. Was her letter proof that she had been making up data to support various paranoid ideas? I couldn't face that possibility. I chose to ignore it when I called my mother again about a week later to tell her about Maria.

My mother decided Thanksgiving would be a good time for her to
head out west for a visit to California. Even though Maria and I were
planning a trip to New York that Christmas, my mother wanted to
scope out for herself exactly who this "Maria" was.

November 2, 1998

Adam—

You're a free agent. So if you want to visit some people
in Jersey, do so. I'd just like to know when you're
coming in and when you're leaving so I can go to the
airport when you leave. Not when you arrive! I'll see
you Christmas Day. That will make me happy. That's
why I thought you'd stay in the city Christmas Day, also
night. I must forewarn you about Bonnie. She is a little
jealous of your girlfriend because even though Bonnie
is your Aunt (remind her), I think she has a crush on
you. Maybe you should tell Maria. My shrink thinks
my whole family are limited people that have serious
problems of their own that have never been resolved.
Talk about a dysfunctional family.

I'm looking forward to meeting Maria and her mother.
I'd love to know where in New York she lives. If she's
near Manhattan, we might be able to meet for lunch one
day. Does she work? Have to get back to work.

Love,

Mom

P.S. I'll see you Thanksgiving. Going to my post office
tomorrow to see if my ticket is there! Can't wait to leave.

Oh, my Lord. My mother has a shrink? My mother wants Maria's
mother's home address? MY AUNT BONNIE HAS A "CRUSH" ON
ME? Jesus! That is some nasty shit! Where the HELL does she come
up with this stuff? It's so random and so out-of-the-blue disturbing!
Could anyone shed a little light on where this could have come from?

I decided to call my aunt Clare. She knows my mother. She knows Bonnie. Maybe she'll get it. "Joannie said that? Listen, dear, I really don't want to get involved in this nonsense."

(I wondered for a second if it was actually Aunt Clare who had a crush on me. Maybe my telling her that my mother thought Aunt Bonnie had a crush on me got her all crazy with jealousy and then she couldn't even talk to me on the phone for another second because all she could think of from that point on was DUEL! Aunt Bonnie!! DUEL! Aunt Bonnie!! DUEL!! Who says I'm not self-obsessed?!)

The day after my mother arrived in LA, Maria decided to meet us at my apartment so we could all head out for a nice dinner. It was the first time they were to come face-to-face. My mother was wearing some sort of strapless top and a skirt that was *waaaay* too short. The whole thing was far too revealing for a woman her age, and inappropriate for meeting someone I really cared about. After Maria's first surprised glance, we all loaded into my car and arrived at the restaurant in no time at all. When we were seated, we shared some pleasant conversation until all of a sudden, out of the friggin' nonlinear blue, my mother proceeded to tell Maria and I an awkwardly provocative story about an experience she had just had in New York. One night, Mom went into the Algonquin Hotel for some drinks. She was sitting at the bar having a lovely time, and about two or three tequila sunrises later, she realized she hadn't brought any money with her. (*Mom, I thought, where is this story going?*) Not knowing what to do, she did the logical thing most responsible and respectable adults with half a conscience would do. She asked where the ladies' room was, proceeded to get up, and left. See ya! Without paying.

After finishing the story, she laughed modestly and asked us if we could believe it.

"Can you believe it?"

Wow. That went well.

I'm pretty sure any other girl might have walked away right then and there. But no hoodlum mother was gonna get in my girl's way. No sirree.

Maria and I decided to wait until Memorial Day weekend to travel to New York. It would be my turn to meet her mother, Annette. And that brought me one of my all time personal favorite letters.

You & Maria are staying near Central Park—Don't go into Park after dark!—

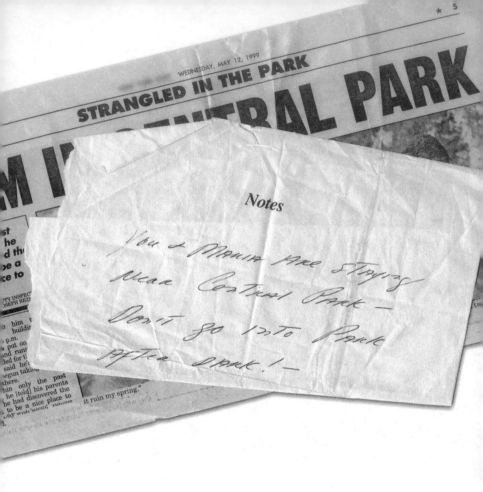

Even the newspaper didn't scare Maria off! She actually fell over laughing.

Fortunately for all of us, it only got weirder.

May 25, 1999
Adam—
<u>Please</u> send me address and phone number where
you'll be staying in New York. Self-addressed envelope
enclosed. (I won't use it. Just like to have it.) Also, let
me know where and what time I'm to meet you. It
doesn't matter as I can take off work anytime. But, I

need to know a couple of days before and I have no
way to contact you so send me address where you'll be
staying so I can feel grounded.
Love,
Mom

I couldn't just call her with the information? No. I needed to send
it to her in a self-addressed, stamped envelope. And why stamped?
Does it make any sense to you?

Did she think I didn't have the thirty-three cents? Note the layers
of carefully crafted guilt: "Please send me address and phone number which I have no intention of ever using because I would never
think of bothering you, even though I'm an elderly woman on a limited income and am only looking to feel grounded by knowing where
you are and where you'll be at any given moment." It was as though
my mother believed all communication was going to end. Perhaps
my return letter would be the LAST time we ever got to exchange information. What are you waiting for? Put it in the mail! Today!

Now let me tell you a little about MARIA'S mom, Annette (*Anto
nia to her Italian friends*). Annette (*Antonia*) is a little sensitive about
the fact that I'm not writing a book about *her*. Granted, she deserves
one, but her relationship with Maria (*though cuckoo nonetheless*) is
completely different from the one I have with my mother. First of
all, there's the obvious fact that theirs is a relationship between two
women. All generalizations aside, it's much more "normal" to hear
about an overprotective mother and daughter arguing all the time
about silly things. And let me say that Maria's mother LIVES to argue about everything, all the time. Annette truly believes she was put
on this planet to take the opposing side to ANYTHING Maria says.
There's no fear. Just opposition for opposition's sake. There's also
never been any documentation of her ramblings, as Maria's mom
does most of her confrontation via the phone or in person.

However, on the day we met, I must say she kept the arguing
down to a bare minimum. The sun was shining; the West Side was

hopping; it was summer in New York and the mozzarella melted in
your mouth before it ever left your hand. We sat inside at a little piz-
zeria where Annette asked me questions about my past, my present,
and my likes and dislikes. She also offered no whacked-out stories
about stealing alcoholic beverages at hotel bars. Yup. This was good.
I thought if I was to end up marrying Maria, parental normalcy just
might find its way into the genes.

June 1999

Adam—

Here's a "20" to have lunch. I hope you have screws on
your windows. On the news, it said "Killer Bees" are
on their way to LA!! Remember that kid you knew in
Miami that said that? Enclosed find check for ticket.

Love,

Mom

July 22, 1999

Adam—

You can win $5,000 in a poetry contest if you buy the
book "The Writer" in any bookstore. In the back, there
is a listing of contests (in back of book). You send your
poems to that address with © on bottom of poems
which indicate they have been copywrited [sic]. You tell
them when you send in poems, that you are sending a
"chapbook." That is what your poems are called. I got all
this information from a published writer I met. I know
you can win the $5,000.

Love,

Mom

Friday

Adam—

My pension # is 320762. I get $200 a month if anything

happens to me. You will be getting the benefit. I
want you to be aware of it. I also have Veteran's Life
Insurance and Mutual of Omaha.
Love,
Mom
P.S. Are you taking care of the tires on both your cars?

I'm building a new life here, Mom . . .

Hadgie—
Do you ever get the FEELING that someone is
THINKING of YOU?
   It's ME!
Love,
Grandma

She's writing to my dog???

Hadgie—
I miss you. I hope you're being a good doggie. Maybe
Adam can buy you a new bone from me.
Love you,
Grandma

"Grandma"? Is my mother "Grandma"? Well, whoever this person is, it sure sounds like they want Maria and me to get pregnant.

Adam—
Got some new fancy checks for my checking account.
Keep them under my mattress. It's safe there.
   Are you and Maria taking precautions against
pregnancy? Once you have a child, your life changes
completely. Make sure you're ready for it.
Love,
Mom

Wait, what? Do you want the kid or not?

Maria and I began planning another trip back east, but began to think twice about it after reading this:

Wednesday

Adam—

If you come here on Labor Day, please don't expect me to meet you at Bonnie's. I haven't heard from her for a year and I want nothing to do with her.

This also applies to the relatives from Jersey that don't even know if I'm alive. You do what you want, but I will see you without any of them. So we'll arrange it.

This is, of course, if you come here. Otherwise, I'll come out there.

If you do come here, you should know that the county that Andrew lives in is on the alert for a serious outbreak of Lyme Disease. So, have him come into New York. It's safer. I'm sure he won't tell you. His wife has it.

All my love—

Mom

This is odd. The relatives from Jersey don't even know if she's alive, yet SHE knows they have Lyme disease.

Well, why risk the plague just for another quick visit? Maria and I rescheduled our plans to go for New Year's Eve.

My mother was working as a social worker for the State of New York. These letters she wrote from her office always make me laugh as my name fit so seamlessly in the box labeled CASE NAME. Oh, the irony...

CASE NAME	ADDRESS	GAT. /OADD. NO. /QUE.
Abram		PAGE NO.

DATE	
10/15/99	I know I worry too much about you — You are so capable I have no reason — When I go off — Just indulge me —
Halloween is coming & I know you are going to be at UCLA — Those college students drink a lot & then drive as you well know — Please wear your seat belts that night & be careful driving! —
You told me about those people at the hotel where you work who indulge in things they should not — Stay away from them! —
And I worry about the guy that was just fired — I hope (Marcus) he's not a crazy person! —
Love
Mom —

Case Name: Adam

10/13/99

I know I worry too much about you—You are so capable
I have no reason—When I go off—just indulge me—

   Halloween is coming & I know you are going to be at
UCLA—Those college students drink a lot & then drive
as you well know—Please wear your seatbelts that night
& be careful driving!—

   You told me about those people at the hotel where
you work who indulge in things they should not—Stay
away from them!—

   And I worry about the guy that was just fired—I hope
(Marcus) he's not a crazy person!—

Love,

Mom

It's as though my mother knew her letters would one day be stud-
ied in psychology classes all over the world. Perhaps a graduate of
one of those classes will find time to explain this one to me.

10/15/99

Pooh-Pooh—

STOP! Did she just call me "Pooh-Pooh"?

When you come East for Xmas—you're going to need
some warm clothes—Not just your winter coat—But—a
good jacket with "down" in it so you could knock around
in it. —Enclosed find jacket from "Land's End" catalogue—
If you'd care to order it, I guess they can deliver it to your
work place so it would be safe—It's best to get it in a large
so you have extra room if you want to wear a sweater—
As soon as I can—I'll send you a $50. so you'll only have
to pay $50. for it. I do NOT think it's a good idea to write

,your credit card # on any order form—Send a check or
money order instead—(If you decide to order—.) Do you
still have the cap and scarf I sent you last year—?—
Look at the boots too for Winter.
Love,
Mom
Don't use your credit card!
  Don't use your credit card
    No credit card

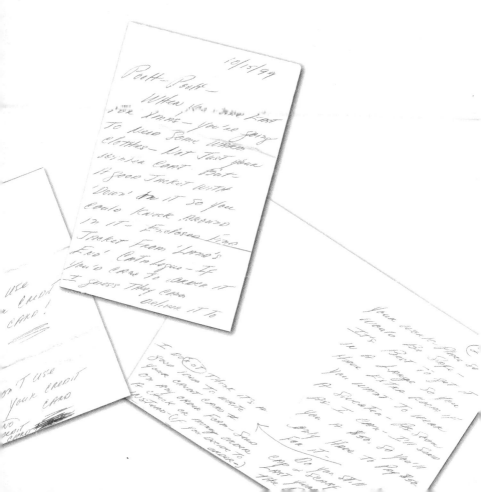

Perhaps the paranoia of that letter could all be chalked up to the panic of Y2K setting in. And was anyone on the planet still using money orders?

Countdown to 2000:

TEN, NINE . . .

November 16, 1999
Chicken—
Here at office. Boring!
    What date are you coming East?
    On what airline?
    What airport?
    Where are you staying?
    What is plane number?
    Am I still spending Christmas Day with all of you at Annette's?
    Where and what time should I meet you?
    What date you going back?
    Do you have warm clothes because it will be bitter cold?
    Christmas is on Saturday. I'm off the 24th and 27th, so I will have 4 whole days. Hope I can spend some time with you.
Much Love,
Mom
P.S. As you know, Nan's birthday is 11/29, Bonnie's 12/23.

My mother wants nothing to do with Bonnie but, by the way, her birthday is December 23.

EIGHT, SEVEN . . .

November 17, 1999

Adam—

Maybe you could eat out Thanksgiving and I'll pick up
tab. Wherever you want to eat. Also, when you and
Maria buy a tree for Christmas, an artificial one is safer
than a real one as a real one can catch on fire with the
electric lights. (I know you think I'm weird.) So?

Love,

Mom

SIX, FIVE . . .

11/18/99

We're preparing a list at work for all our clients who
would be at risk should electricity in New York stop
because of the Y2K problem Jan. 31, 2000 [sic]—This
means No Traffic Lights—No Mass Transportation—No
Phones or Refrigeration—No Lights—No Elevators—

So—the thought occurred to me—don't drive that
night & don't take elevators—Keep a flash-light on
hand—and have some canned food in apt.—Don't go on
sub-ways—Stay near where you're staying so you can
walk back to apartment. You need bottled water and a
manual can opener. When you get to apartment where
you're staying, get prepared just in case of emergency.
See what you need.

This is not your hysterical mother talking. We have
been so instructed at work by a well-informed computer
expert!!!!

Better to take precaution than be sorry.

Love,

Mom

I love the fact that she's got the wrong date for Y2K. She's planning for Armageddon a month too late!

FOUR, THREE . . .

Monday
November 22, 1999
Adam—
In the year 2000, don't go up in a plane New Year's Eve and don't go on an elevator! Those are only the 2 things to avoid until we see how computers are working.
Love,
Mom

TIME IS RUNNING OUT!

TWO . . .

November 23, 1999
Just a reminder:
Over the holidays, it would be a good idea to wear your seatbelt.
Love,
Mom
And don't ever go down to where I'm staying under any circumstances.

RED-RUM! RED-RUM!

ONE . . .

11/29/99
Adam—
Enclosed find a little Hanukah gelt—which means

ADVERTISEMENT

SPECIAL ADVERTISING SUPPLEMENT

PREPARING FOR Y2K

Get a ...

& Hand operated can opener. For Apt. That

... with mal.

Jim Lord, an informational technologies expert, raised an ... question. "What is ... for over-preparing ... there is ...

juices and fruits, spices and condiments.

General Telephone advised it's customers to set aside two weeks of cash. The Red Cross has since advised the same. Others have recommended ... including cash sufficient to pay ... of bills, where ... six months' ... need-

enough. It is ironic that this administration, that prides itself on being so high tech, is not really facing up to the potential disaster that is down the road a little bit. If Y2K triggers an economic and Government collapse, it may well be the vice president who suffers - imagine Al Gore's spending the entire election campaign explaining why he did not foresee the crisis."

... the previous year, ... Chief ... for the ...

... the ... codes ... tem's ... d (not ... way). ... of the ... up the ... the time. ... an tested. ... sted means ... nt.

You're staying at a 3 day supply of water — Take all your medications

11/18/99

We're preparing a list at
work for all our clients
who would be at risk
should electricity in New York
stop because of the
Y2K problem Jan. 1, 2000 —
means no traffic lights —
mass transportation —
phones or refrigeration —
lights — no elevators —
The thought occurred to
Don't drive that night
don't take elevators — keep
flash-light on hand — & have
canned food in apt. —
on sub-ways — stay near
you're staying so you can

money—Use it to buy whatever—
   Spoke with Annette—We're supposed to meet one day
next week & go to a comedy club—
Love,
Joan—
Ooops
Mom—

I DON'T EVEN KNOW WHO I AM BUT I'M HEADING TO THE
BOMB SHELTER! GOTTA GO! AAAAAAAAAAAAAAAAAAH!!!!!
HAPPY NEW YEAR!!!!!

11/29/99

Happy —

Enclosed find Beth's

Enclosed homework money —

Little phones To pay whhat—

which it Time To

Use with Time To

open — notice next

Notice composed next to A

proposal —

It was time to quit my job as a travel agent and take a position as the manager of a piano store in LA. Good environment, better benefits, and nobody there knew my mother.

Yet.

This Capricorn horoscope she sent me from *Glamour* magazine seemed to predict that good things would be coming my way.

His Sign

Capricorn Man He's reputed to have the strongest sex drive in the zodiac. But he's also very practical and has "marriage material" stamped on his forehead. **If You're Interested, Do** be a good girl in public—and a bad girl behind closed doors. If he says 8:00 P.M., be ready to go by 7:45. He's superpunctual. **If You're Interested, Don't** tell him about seeking revenge on your ex—he's far too discreet to approve of such behavior. **Best Matches** Scorpio and Taurus **Worst Matches** Aries and Gemini **Celebrity Goats** Nicolas Cage, Kevin Costner, Cuba Gooding Jr., Ricky Martin

Then the following letter came not long after. By the way, thanks, Mom! Maria is a Gemini.

Thurs.

Adam—

1. I had NO idea that was on the horoscope—I didn't even remember what Maria's B'day was—(I only read the cute saying they had)—

2. If you want me to be the "Bad" guy in this for something "harmless"—then—so be it—I can't control what people think! If I bothered to look at that part of the clipping—I may have thought twice. But, it was so unimportant to me. I never even looked! Maria should know in her heart how very much I care for her!

3. If you still have the cold after the antibiotics stop, you should have the doctor renew them 'cause I had to renew mine when I had the flu. You have to stay on 1 week longer. It's so cold up here now. I had to put on my heavy "down" coat 'cause I don't want to get sick again. Take Care.

Love,

Mom

Who reads these horoscopes? Why is my mother mailing horoscopes? Needless to say, Maria was a little pissed. After all, who are we mere mortals to argue with Venus and Mars? The stress of managing the problem of my mother was becoming more than I could handle.

February 11, 2000
Pooh-Pooh—

[*Heavy sigh.*]

I'm at the office and have very little to do as I have
not been going in field as often as I should as I've been
feeling so tired lately. I'm going right home after work.
  On the 19th of this month, I will send you $100. Use it
to buy groceries for the week.
  Try not to put chemicals in your system, like Prozac.
If your grandfather were here (on your father's side),
he'd tell you not to put that in your body.
  I hope you're making progress in your search. Did the
piano job in that hotel come through? Don't they have
any clubs in Sherman Oaks that need a piano player?
Love,
Mom

Yes, at this point Pooh-Pooh needed Prozac. After meeting with
a few doctors and explaining my situation, they gladly handed me a
lifetime prescription for Lexapro.

Sunday
Adam & Maria—
Sitting in Laundromat waiting for wash. Chore day.
Did you two ever take out Homeowner's insurance?
When was the last time you had a tetanus shot? You're
supposed to have one every 10 years. Speak to your
doctor about it and see what he says. Some people just
wait until they step on a nail or get bitten by a dog. But
if you get one every 10 years, you don't need to. I had
mine 5 years ago.
  I know you both think I'm nuts, I don't care. Life isn't
easy and I do the best I can, like we all do.
  If my finances come together as I plan, I'll be making
my reservation for LA. The beginning of March, I'll call
Michael [boss of the travel agency] 'cause he gets me the
one on computer so I don't need ticket.

Am dating a lawyer now who is in his late 50's. A
youngor man. Very interesting and puts a little pizzaz
[sic] into my otherwise mundane life!
Love,
Mom

Maria and I hadn't given tetanus much thought, but we were
willing to make a date night out of it. (*Anything for the new prospective head of the CDC!*) I wondered what made my mother think of
tetanus in the first place. Perhaps that lawyer in his late fifties she
was dating contracted it. I don't know. We never did hear anything
about *him* again.

Dear Adam—
This sweater was bought on the sidewalk of New York
for $2. If it's no good, don't worry. Give it to Hadgie to
sit on in his bed!
Love,
Mom

A thought: Wouldn't that $2 sweater from the New York sidewalk
most likely carry some form of tetanus? Although if I had it cleaned, I
bet it would look snazzy for a few job interviews . . .

Case Name: Adam
April 28, 2000
Suggestion
Go to some of the Major Motion Picture Studios.
(Paramount, MGM, etc.) They have a personnel office.
Take your resume and speak to one of the officers and
tell them you're looking for a job related to music. What
openings do they have. Sometimes, they need in-house
musicians and you have to go (in person), 'cause once
they see how GORGEOUS you are, all the people will

help you in your pursuit. It won't hurt to go as they do
have a personnel department there.

Love,

Mom

And then conserve your money for necessary items only.
   Please let me know if you're going to fly off
somewhere. I would want to know what plane you're on.

How insane is that? People would see me, pass out from my stunning good looks, and instantly offer me a high-paying job. I can hear them in HR now! "Where DOES he buy his sweaters . . . ?"

A few months later, I called my mother to tell her that I had decided to ask Maria to be my wife. Then I got this:

November 13, 2000

Adam—

Enclosed is some insurance I'm taking out, if I get killed
by accident at no cost to me. Only $1,000, but, what the
hell. It's free. Need you to know as I hope you have list of
all other insurances. Mutual of Omaha—$15,000. Work,
City of NY—$10,000. Veterans Life—$10,000. Pension
Plan—$2,000 (or more).

   By the way, I'm very happy about what you told me on
the phone last Wednesday night! I think you've made a
good choice!

Love,

Mom

"By the way"? She "thinks" I made a good choice? Wow. Talk about an overwhelming endorsement. My future wife is "good." Well, in the plus column, Mom's death payout has ballooned to $38,000.

That's up $8,000 from the former $30K! We could have ourselves a helluva engagement party!

For Christmas, Maria and I planned a trip to New York where I devised a scheme to keep Maria and her family in the dark about my nuptial plans. I searched for the most perfect vintage-looking engagement ring I could find and started to get very excited about the whole thing! I did my best to keep all negative energy away from me for just a little while longer...

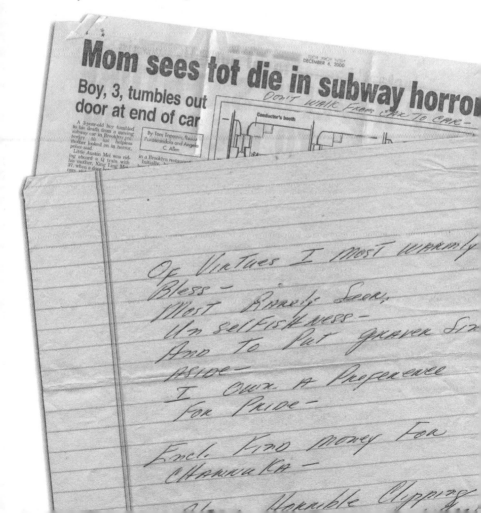

Mom sees tot die in subway horror

DECEMBER 6, 2000

Boy, 3, tumbles out door at end of car

DON'T WALK FROM CAR TO CAR—

Conductor's booth

A 3-year-old boy tumbled to his death from a moving subway car in Brooklyn yesterday, as his helpless mother looked on in horror, police said.

Little Austin Mei was riding aboard a Q train with his mother, Xing Ling Mei, 37, when a door

By Toni Tepovic, Russia Purascondola and Angelo C. Allen

in a Brooklyn restaurant. Initially, h...

Of Virtues I most warmly
Bless —
Most Ramaly Seeks,
Unselfishness —
And to Put graven Sin
Aside —
I own A Preference
For Pride —

Encl. Find money for
Chanukah —

Also Horrible Clipping...

December 6, 2000
Of Virtues I most warmly bless—
Most rarely seen,
Unselfishness—
And to put graver sins aside,
I own a preference for pride.
    Enclosed find money for Channuka [*sic*].
    Also—Horrible clipping of what happens when you
walk thru cars on subways. You could fall on tracks!
Don't walk thru cars!
Love,
Mom
P.S. I decided <u>NOT</u> to take out additional insurance with
Chase Bank as I had told you.

Shit! Like a dropping stock. Now Mom's only worth $37,000.
[*Back of envelope*]

<u>Make sure</u> you have a warm coat & hat—Before you
come East!

Now my humiliation couldn't even be hidden from the mail carrier!

When Pop-the-Big-Question Day finally arrived, I ran over to Maria's father's workplace in the middle of a chilly December New York afternoon. I'm an old-fashioned kind of guy, and felt that I had to ask for his permission to marry his daughter. When I ran all the way across town to meet him and opened my mouth to say the words, he shook my hand, and said he thought Maria and I would make a wonderful couple. That was it? OK. What did I expect! I said my thank-yous and ran all the way back across town to get to the Helmsley Park Lane Hotel, where I told Maria we should meet.

The story was that my good friend Ben and his fiancée were staying there for the night, and wanted to hook up with us for dinner. I arranged it with the front desk manager to register our room in Ben's name.

When Maria knocked on the door of "Ben's" hotel room, I escorted her in. There was a view of Central Park, a dozen roses, and a bottle of nice champagne. There was also no Ben and no fiancée. Maria asked what was going on. She could tell I was up to something as she allowed me to lead her to the couch that was centered right beneath the picturesque window.

I took out a little cassette player (*now THAT sounds ancient*) and pressed PLAY. "Another Suitcase in Another Hall" filled the room. I proceeded to get down on one knee, took out the ring, and asked her to be my wife. Thankfully, she said yes.

The next morning, we told our mothers the big news at breakfast. My mother had a somewhat stunned look on her face for most of that day, even though I had told her of my plans a while back. Maria and I didn't stay in New York long enough to figure it out, but I knew I'd learn the truth soon enough. Later that night, Maria and I flew back to LA to begin making our wedding plans. A few days later, I got the "reason" in the mail. What was REALLY on my mother's mind on that cold New York day? You're not going to believe this.

December 30, 2000

Adam—

I don't understand why you or Maria couldn't see that your coat was not a <u>winter</u> coat! If you had a coat with "down" in it, you would never have gotten a cold. They sell them at Champs near Peter's where you were staying for $50. Seeing how cold it was, why didn't you go there?

Michael's birthday is January 10. It's up to you if you want to call. I thought about inviting him to the wedding and I don't think it's a good idea. He could cause a scene easily. I was just thinking of Nan when I said Yes at first. But, you can talk to her and explain (beforehand) why you can't afford to invite him since he may ruin your wedding! Besides, no one would be willing for him to stay in their home, including Bonnie.

As for Pop, he would not cause a scene and I do think he should be invited. He would be very hurt if you don't invite him and he will find out as there are cousins I have that will make sure he knows plus he reads all the papers. And since you have kept in contact with him, he would definitely expect it from you. I would talk to Nan and she would be very civil about it. But, I'm sure even she would agree he should be invited.

Take care of you both.

Love,

Mom

P.S. Why do you have to go to Miami in January? Why don't you wait till February or March? You were just away. Give yourself a chance to catch up! Save some of your money or at least wait until you get the money from Pop. Tell me if you haven't gotten it in a week.

Of course. It was my winter coat. It all made sense to me now. That whole morning at breakfast in New York worrying about what flulike bacteria would creep into my bagel and cream cheese because of my foolish laissez-faire attitude. Not one single mention of the fact that—just two days earlier—I had asked my girlfriend to marry me. Nope. And friggin' UNCLE MICHAEL. How'd HE turn into the star of the letter?

Maria and I set the date for the Fall of 2001.

Planning a wedding can be costly no matter what. Then there's the question of who to invite, who should sit next to whom, what people will and won't eat, what type of music to have at the party (*can you believe KC and the Sunshine Band wanted to charge me $50,000 to play the reception?*), what to wear, where to have it, etc. One of the biggest concerns for my mother was who from our family should be left off the guest list.

Friday
Adam—
Let Michael think he's coming to the wedding. When he doesn't get an invitation, he'll know. When you're down there, let him have the illusion. If you want to tell Nan, that's different.
    Remember to go near a lifeguard if you go near the beach. There's a big undertow in the Florida waters.
Love,
Mom

Ah, that Michael. Like a Great White barreling toward me. And . . . cue theme from *Jaws* . . . !

March 5, 2001
Wednesday
Adam,

When you see Michael, don't confront him with
anything. Just say Hello and stay away from him. He
and Nan live in their own world of their making. It's not
up to us to change something that works for them. Even
if we don't agree with it.

When I was there, I just let him talk and didn't
comment.

How can you comment on fantasy? He is a very sick
individual. If he were my son, I would put him in a
structured setting where no harm could come to him
and where he could do no harm. Nan likes to pretend
he's normal. I'm sure she really knows he's not.

I just worry about you and Maria being anywhere
near him since I know he is so jealous of you because
of the way Nan brags about you. Since he's not in his
right mind, I don't know what he's capable of. Be careful.
Stay away from him and don't challenge him. And don't
accept any drinks from him. He has a whole supply of
narcotics in his room.

I know I sound like a book from Steven [*sic*] King, but
believe me. I made a big mistake by staying there on
my vacation. I was not able to afford a hotel. I shouldn't
have gone. It was a nightmare and I had no sleep there
as he's up all night. I won't do it again. I just wanted to
see Nan as I haven't seen her in 2 years.
Love,
Mom

Forget all the talk about lifeguards and undertows and fantasy
and normalcy. My mother confessed to sounding like Stephen King!
This was a huge victory for my team of analysts. It's been clear to me
all along that my mother needed help. I knew she'd been seeing a
shrink in New York for quite some time. I wondered if HE was seeing
any changes in her. I wondered if HE was seeing a shrink! And what

were his credentials, anyway? And why did it seem like my mother was not making any progress?

Saturday
Adam—
I was thinking how long ago I had a tetanus shot and for me, it's been about 5 years. I don't know when you had a tetanus shot. Do you? I know you're supposed to have one every 10 years. Has it been 10 years for you? I know you had one in California. Do you remember the doctor that gave it to you? You could call and ask how long ago you had it if you know who gave it to you.
Love,
Mom

Was this letter recycled? Notable Tetanus Fact. Traveller, General Robert E. Lee's favorite horse, once stepped on a nail and died of tetanus.

March 19, 2001
Adam—
When is Maria's birthday? I forgot and I want to send her a gift so make sure you tell me.
    Don't forget to file your taxes before April 15th. Get all your stuff together.
    I'm sitting and waiting for my shrink as I got here too early.
    Take care and please make sure you're getting some rest.
    Working 6 days a week is no joke.
    How are the plans going for the wedding? No one tells me anything.
Love,
Mom

When's Maria's birthday? You know goddamn well you didn't miss it because she's a GEMINI! Remember?

I can almost see the dim light from the mauve table lamp near the pile of plastic-covered magazines. My mother sits alone in the small doctor's office. There are no windows. It was just carpeted. She feels safe here as she flicks up the tiny metal switch near the only other door in the room. That door is closed, but will soon open to a familiar face, which will welcome her in. The doctor knows my mother's early. She's always early. She sits herself down in one of those two comfy chairs and, for a moment, stares out into space. My mother has some time to kill, and she's inspired. She pulls out a pen from her purse, a blank piece of paper, and begins to write:

April 11, 2001
To Whom It May Concern:
I, Joan, leave everything I have to my son, Adam,
including anything that is bequeathed to me. My
insurance policies have Adam as beneficiary and any
balance in my checking account along with the money
that is available in my pension fund at work are to go to
Adam.
Joan

Adam—
This is a legal document. Please put it with all your
important papers. Wherever you keep them. Should
be in a safe deposit box. I gave you a copy of my Will. I
don't know where you put it. It was many years ago. You
should be organized with all documents.
    So, you're prepared if need be.
    (I only say this because I'm guilty of not being

organized and I don't know where anything is!)
Mom

Oh, trust me! I know where EVERYTHING is! In fact, what do you say we make this book a legal document?

7/8/2010

7/08/10

EMMA J. AYALA
Commission # 1835823
Notary Public - California
Los Angeles County
My Comm. Expires Feb 9, 2013

There. Now it's official.

Back to the matter at hand. It was time for the $10,000 question: Should UNCLE MICHAEL be invited to my wedding? Maria asked me if UNCLE MICHAEL would really make the trip from Miami to New York. I figured he wouldn't. And since he'd find out about the wedding from Nan, why not invite him?! He's not all THAT bad! Maybe he'd even "buy" us a nice piece of jewelry as a wedding present.

April 13, 2001
From: Mom
Subject: Adam
Sitting at my desk. Have some time.

When are you and Maria going to Miami? Where are you staying? Don't tell Nan where you're staying 'cause she'll tell Michael and he'll show up there. You don't want that. Also, don't drive him anywhere. He's bad news. Say you don't have time. And don't tell HIM he's not being invited. He'll find out later on. No need to upset him. Please understand he's unbalanced and you don't need to create negative energy while you're in town. Be neutral.
Love,
Mom

"Well, honey," I said to Maria, "let's think about it. My mother IS right that we really should surround ourselves with nothing but happy thoughts ..."

Monday
Adam—
You were 9 years old & playing Superman & crashed thru the front glass door of the house in Wayne—We had to rush you to emer. room & you had stitches in your arm—This terrible article encl. shows you how you have

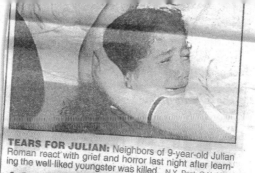

TEARS FOR JULIAN: Neighbors of 9-year-old Julian Roman react with grief and horror last night after learning the well-liked youngster was killed. N.Y. Post: G.N. Miller

'Superman' boy dies in Bronx rooftop plun...

By ERIKA MARTINE...
LARRY C...

o...
to
ting
"Hi
said,
before
across,
tendent
The lo
lian's bo
ground br
into the co
they found
scene. "He
his left side. Y
his bones were
the whole si
body," neighbor
lison said.
Bojang,
12

Mom,

Adam—

You were 9 yrs. old + plays...
Superman + busstee than Th...
Front glass door of the Hou...
in Wayne — We Had to rea...
you to emer. room + you n...
stitches in your arm — This...
Terrible article Encl. Sh...
you How you Have to wo...
Kids so — luckily we li...
on ground Floor —
       I Had a lovely Dr...
Annette yesterday! I Sa...
The place where Annemarie...
Be! So Beautiful! —
       Annette Told me To...
you know I want A...
       Sent To: Terry
             c/o Jo...

to watch kids so—Luckily we lived on ground floor.

I had a lovely day with Annette yesterday! I saw the place where wedding will be! So beautiful!

Annette told me to let you know I want an invitation sent to: Jerry

(over)

And please let me have a say as to who will be sitting at my table. I don't care about other tables.

Do you have a Rabbi that will be at the Church?

I saw the Church. It's beautiful! Remember, you could always call "Rent a Rabbi" in New York.

My Love,

Mom

Wednesday

Adam & Maria—

You shouldn't go to South America on your Honeymoon. I was just watching news on TV and the militia in Columbia [sic] just kidnapped some more Americans. They have been doing this in parts of South America and it is not safe there. It is not safe in Israel either. Hawaii is safe. Please don't put yourself in harm's way when you're just starting out together!

Love,

Mom

P.S. You're supposed to have a tetanus shot every 10 years. When was your last one given? I think I asked you before.

South America? Colombia? Israel? For God's sake, we were talking about going to Sedona for our honeymoon. That or perhaps visiting the Peaks of Otter Lodge in Virginia, where I'm told Robert E. Lee's favorite horse once stepped on a nail and died of tetanus.

But wait! As if all the above wasn't enough . . .

May 13, 2001
Adam & Maria—
You said Michael probably won't come to wedding. But,
Nan had told me he was coming and he'll probably stay
at Nancy and Richard's house in Livingston and Nancy
and Richard aren't even being invited! Don't send him
an invitation or he will come! Why would you take a
chance when your wedding is sooo special!!!? He does
not know how to act in a social situation and I have
enough to do. Keeping an eye on Pop 'cause I don't know
how he'll react when he sees Nan after 50 years. If
they're at same table and he starts being abusive, I may
have to move Nan to another table. (He's close to being
senile, so you don't know.)
Love,
Mom

Hank (*Pop*) is my maternal grandfather. A superstar sportsman
who lived in Bayonne, New Jersey, he divorced my grandmother long
before I was born, and she married the man I grew up knowing and
loving as my grandfather. Mel. Little did I know (*not until my senior
year of high school*) that (*surprise!*) Mel wasn't my "blood" grandfather. No, no. My "Pop" in "Joisey" (*who never remarried and allegedly
liked the occasional whore*) was. Go figure. Sure, I wanted him at my
wedding. But there was my mother with her letter, filling my head
with the obligatory commentary one needs to hear right before his
wedding. You know, I'm beginning to wonder if my mother is really
my mother.

Adam—
Dementia is when the brain has deteriorated and the
person cannot function rationally. So anything Pop
says is questionable. So, Stay Away from him before the
wedding 'cause he's trouble with a capital T.

I've tried to hire a reputable woman for him but he'd
rather have his prostitutes! His friends (Frank, the
Barber) told me to stay away from him and concentrate
on my own life. They all know he's weird! Don't worry,
if he goes to wedding, Nan and I will gag and bind him!
We'll take care of him.
Mom

If only pay-per-view had existed then. And talk about the pot calling the kettle black . . .

August 20, 2001
Adam & Maria—
If you go to the beach on Labor Day, make sure you don't
swim far from shore because there are undertows in
the Pacific and being a good swimmer is not enough to
deal with that. So, be careful. Please. I know you're both
grown adults, but I'm just reminding you to be careful.
Love,
Mom
You probably don't have time to go to the beach, anyhow.

Undertows. If only they remained the worst thing in the world.
Because then September 11 happened. If there was ever a single human being in this world who did not need a September 11 to inten-
sify her lifelong relationship with fear, mistrust, tragedy, and grief, it
was my mother. The fact that the catastrophe happened right before
Maria and I were to be married, *in* New York City, was the icing on
the wedding cake. It raised my mother's calamity meter by infinity.
While it wasn't easy for anyone to be positive about anything after
that day, Maria and I, like many people, chose to continue on with
our lives as best as we could. We were truly excited about getting
married, and nothing was going to change that.
    As it turned out, neither UNCLE MICHAEL nor Hank came to the

wedding, though Hank did end up giving us a large chunk of money to help pay for it.

Our wedding day turned out to be a beautiful day in New York. I actually have a picture of my mother hugging one of my first cousins (*formerly known as an "evil" relative*) at the reception. Maybe the catastrophe of September 11 put everything else into perspective. Maybe this was the time when all fear needed to be put aside in order for us to survive.

When Maria and I were introduced as husband and wife at our reception, we walked into that room with our heads held high and a plan to live out our life together to its fullest. For now, nothing else mattered but Maria. *Maria.* And suddenly that name would never be the same to me.

4.
Adam's
Family

There was a new Mrs. Chester in town. No doubt THAT would take a little getting used to. When Maria and I (*Mrs. Chester and I*), returned from our honeymoon, this was the FIRST letter I received from my mother (*that OTHER Mrs. Chester...*):

Tuesday

Adam—

I know you had a tetanus shot 10 years ago. I don't know if you've had one since. Ask your doctor. But, I think you're supposed to have one every 10 years.

Love,

Mom

P.S. If anything ever happens to me, Nan will have to go live with Bonnie or go into a nursing home. No one can do it 24/7. She needs constant care and she's incompetent to function on her own. She'll destroy anyone she's with (in her quiet way). She'll be best with Bonnie 'cause Bonnie isn't home that much and there's nowhere she can go to get into trouble.

Tetanus again? Come on! I started wondering if my mother had Alzheimer's. I wasn't sure. But either way, her Stupid-Pet-Names-for-Adam disease was still in full force.

January 28, 2002
Chicken Livers—
I never hear from you two. What's happening? Where are my pictures? If I don't call, you don't call me. Should I stop calling altogether? It wouldn't hurt for you two to call once a week to say Hi! Are you getting enough rest, Adam? 'Cause you seem to be working all the time. Don't burn the candle at both ends. Try to go to bed early once in a while.
Love,
Mom

Chicken Livers, my ass. How long could I take this? Weren't we somewhat past the "I-recognize-I've-got-a-problem" phase? How many Lexapros can a person take at once?

Hello—
Adam—
I know you would agree with this saying in regard to me!
Love,
Mom

The thought had crossed my mind that my mother knew more than she wanted to reveal.

Sunday
Adam,
I sent you $20 at your home. You never mentioned it. Here's a little extra for your pocket.
Love,
Mom

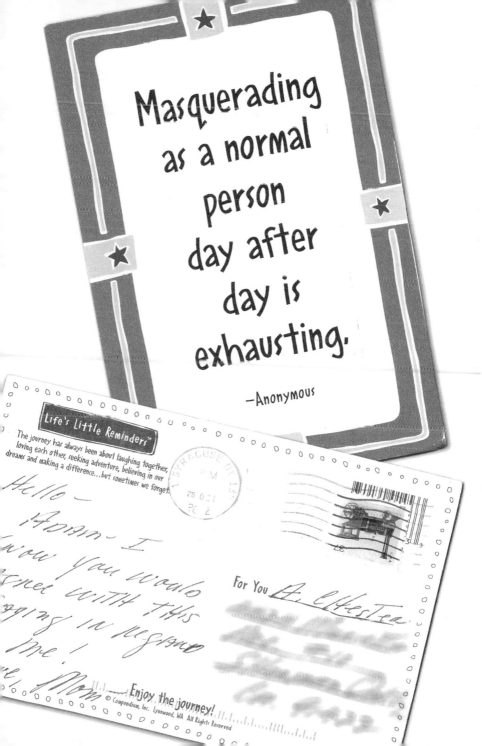

Masquerading
as a normal
person
day after
day is
exhausting.

—Anonymous

Life's Little Reminders™

The journey has always been about laughing together,
loving each other, seeking adventure, believing in our
dreams and making a difference...but sometimes we forget.

Hello—

Mom— I
know you would
agree with this
going in regard
me!

Love, Mom

Enjoy the journey!
© Compendium, Inc. Lynnwood, WA All Rights Reserved

For You A. Chester

P.S. Don't get involved with Pop's business. And don't
sign anything regarding his business! I know what I'm
talking about.

What "business"? What did my mother know? She stopped living
with Pop when she was, what . . . three years old? Thanks, but you can
stop trying to protect me from Pop's posse and his covert ties with
the underworld .

May 7, 2002
I will take out large insurance policy before I get on
airplane, since you're beneficiary. There's also—
   1. Veteran's Life—$10,000
   2. Mutual of Omaha—$15,000
   3. Pension Money—?—From retirement fund HRA 180
Water Street, New York, NY
   No burial—want to be cremated. Less expensive—only
$500. Ashes over the Pacific.
   I know I'm a little nuts. So what?
   Love you both—
   Enjoy each other.

Wait! $10K plus $15K is $25,000, less $500. Holy shit! That's
$24,500! What happened to the $37,000? And I love the "Enjoy each
other." Didn't she mean to add "WHILE THERE'S TIME BEFORE
YOU DANCE ON MY GRAVE, FUCKERS!"?

Tuesday
Adam—
Enclosed find $50 just for you. I sent $100 money order
last week to your house. Did you get it? It was for your
anniversary [sic].
Love,
Mom

(over)
Have you ever heard of Famous Artists? Anyhow, I
spoke with Mr. Bernthal who is the creator. He said to
find out who the manager of the LA Philharmonic is
and call him and ask him if the Philharmonic can play
one of your pieces at the Pop concerts that they put on.
They sometimes do this. Also, Mr. Bernthal, who was
also head of the music department at Syracuse, said for
me to tell him who manager is because if he knows him,
he'll make sure your compositions are played by the LA
Philharmonic.

When I showed that letter to a friend of mine, he Photoshopped
the following image together for me.

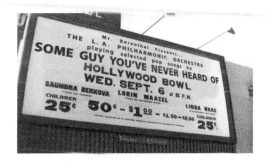

Nice, huh? In the realm of my mother's mind, this makes perfect
sense. If she saw that sign, she'd probably still be leaving messages
with the *Los Angeles Times* asking why they didn't cover it. (*I know I
do sometimes.*)

In my first two years of marriage, my mother made it a point to visit us in California for the holidays. Though it was her constant need
to remind us of her desire to provide for us when she was gone that
always made us feel safe and secure.

Adam—

If something happens to me on plane, you should know
in addition to plane insurance—will take it out at airport.
It's Travelex Omaha NE 11717 Burt Street for $300,000.

    1. Veteran's Life—$10,000

    2. Work—$10,000—insurance policy

    3. United of Omaha—$15,000

    4. Pension at work—$2,000 or $3,000—You're
beneficiary.

    My rent is all paid up so don't let her tell you
otherwise. She's greedy. Take things from my room, 67
Taylor Street, Staten Island. No one has this address.
Don't ever come here except if something happens to
me. It's a Bad neighborhood. Be aware!

    If I'm not around, just enjoy. I don't want you feeling
bad. I'll be happy knowing you're having fun.

Mom

That's 300 plus 10 plus 15 plus . . . *whew*! We're having fun now!

I'd love to hear from some of the residents of this area in Staten
Island. Are you really living in a constant state of fear, anxiety, and
jeopardy? Could you use some donations to help better your town?
I mean, I might be getting some serious cash soon. Seriously. My
mother flies on airplanes a LOT!

Keep This in
case Plane
crashes — It's
for Round Trip —
You get $300,000.
Use it well —
Mom —

CUSTOMER'S RECEIPT

SEE BACK OF THIS RECEIPT
FOR IMPORTANT CLAIM
INFORMATION

NOT
NEGOTIABL

$300,000

Travelex / 205. Services

Omaha, Ne. —

Flight, 205. —

YEAR, MONTH, DAY
2002-11-20

POST OFFICE
331190

AMOUNT
$ 17.00

Maria and I bought our very first house in 2003 when she was
pregnant with our first child. My mother was thinking about leaving
New York again and hooking up with my grandmother since, sadly,
UNCLE MICHAEL passed away suddenly from pulmonary edema.
My grandmother was not handling it well. After all, the two of them
had been living together for more than ten years! (*Remember this for
later!*) My mother decided that she would pick up my grandmother
in Miami, and like an elderly version of Thelma and Louise, the two
of them would move together to Las Vegas, of all places. I realized
Las Vegas was dangerously close to me in California, but I didn't
mind now that I was focused on having our first child.

This letter came to us about a month or so before Maria gave birth.
Keep in mind that we lived about five minutes away from the hospital.

Tuesday
Adam—
When the time comes and you have to drive Maria to
the hospital, make sure you don't go through yellow
lights as you have to get her there in one piece. Your
Dad drove me very slowly when it was my time and it's
good to go for a trial run to see how long it takes obeying
all the lights!
Love,
Mom

We had a boy in the fall of 2003 and we named him Truman Eliot.
Our mothers flew out to meet him not long after he was born.

As a lot of you probably know, life completely changes when you
have a child. Your priorities completely shift. If you have a bad day
at work, you could drive all the way home just as pissed as you were
when you left the office. But the second you walk through your front
door and see your child's face looking up at you, all of that stupid
shit becomes just that: stupid shit that all disappears. Everything's
OK again, and that's when you realize the profound positive energy

being a parent gives you. I wondered how I ended up being as normal as I am, having a mother who was always so worried or scared or focused on the negatives. I vowed that I would never be that way for Truman. I cradled him in my arms and sang "How Deep Is Your Love" by the Bee Gees until he fell asleep. (*Or at least until he pretended to be asleep so I would stop singing the Bee Gees.*) Our house became that party of the new millennium that never seemed to stop! And it was all about positive goodness!

Adam—
This insurance I took out is only for $5,000. But it will cover my burial, as I want to be cremated and ashes to go over Pacific Ocean.
Love,
Mom

According to a previous letter, cremations were five HUNDRED?! Now I'm really confused. Wait! Who cares? Accentuate the positive! I'm a daddy now!

And that happiness kept many people we knew celebrating long after Truman was born. Garçon, please! Cake and ice cream for EVERYONE!

Wed.
Hey—
Last night I bought a pint of ice cream from a local market & after 2 spoonfuls I swallowed a wad of chewed tobacco & spit out a little—Anderson Dairy (after I called them) picked up the specimen to have it tested & would let me know the results. Can you believe it?
Love,
Mom
Let me know what the eye Dr. had to say.
Also—enclosed find some recipes for Maria—

Wed.

Hey – LAST NIGHT
I Bought A Pint of
Ice Cream from A Local
Market & After 2 Spoon-
fuls I Swallowed A Wad
of Chewed Tobacco & Spit
out A Little – Anderson
Dairy (After I called them)
picked up The Specimen
To Have iT Tested & would
let me Know The Resu-
Can you Believe iT?
Love –
Mom –

LeT me Kn
WHAT THE e
DR. HAD TO

Also – Enclosed Fino, Some
Recipes For Maria –

My mother. The twenty-first century's Good Humor Man. Could there really have been chewed tobacco in her ice cream? I didn't think so. But Baskin-Robbins could use a thirty-second flavor . . .

Poisoned by the "wad" and all, my mother still managed to send us a little extra money here and there.

It was a nice thought, considering my wife's Italian heritage.

Maria and I were engulfed in discovering everything there was to know about babies. And while we were busy changing diapers, my mother seemed to be busy robbing the cradle itself.

Wednesday
Adam—
I met a 44-year-old man today at a café. Very attractive!
He came over to my table and sat himself down while I
was having an espresso. He asked me out on a date. Can
you believe it? Anyhow, I'm seeing him Friday night and
don't ask me anything about my date. I just wanted to
inform you that some people regard me in a different
view than you do. So there!
Love,
Mom

It's odd how my mother insisted on informing me that various men from the ages of 18 to 120 were attracted to her. Why is this my business? Wherever she went, there would be someone somewhere who just had to have a piece of that! Now, seriously, my mother used to be a stunning woman. People often compared her to a young Marilyn Monroe.

Today, right now, it's a different story. She's seventy-something years old, walks with a cane, and wears " I ♥ NY" pajama bottoms out in public. Not exactly qualifications for centerfold material, but hey, different strokes. (*I didn't mean that.*)

Tuesday
Adam—
I just finished up with the Department of Motor Vehicles
and the guy who snapped my picture asked me if I was
Eva Maria [*sic*] Saint, the movie star. Just thought I'd
let you know.
Love,
Mom

Fine. I shall suspend my disbelief.

How about *this* for a Christmas greeting? Or, actually, a birthday present, since I was born on Christmas Day.

December 22, 2003
To Whom It May Concern—
This being my Last Will, I leave everything I own, bank
accounts included, to my son, Adam, and I appoint him
executor of my Will. If, God forbid, he predeceases me, I
then leave everything to my Grandson, Truman. Being
of sound mind, I sign this,
Joan

She may not have a dime to her name during the course of any day, but damn it, when she croaks, that shit is mine. (*Or my son's, if I drop dead first.*) Happy Birthday to me, and Merry Christmas to all! P.S. Doesn't anybody have to verify the "Being of sound mind" part?

Regardless, I realized that Truman was now in line for the mother lode. Good for him. To be his age and know there was nothing to ever worry about must be a good feeling. I started worrying at a very young age. I remember the day in fourth grade when I was watching a school play from the audience and asked the kid next to me why the stage looked all blurry. He said that was a stupid question. Turned out I was nearsighted and needed glasses. I told the optometrist that I wouldn't care about having to wear them if I could buy Elton John's glasses.

Unfortunately, according to my mother, reproductions were all sold out.

As karma would have it, years later I became close friends with Davey Johnstone. He's been the lead guitarist for Elton John since 1971, and is now the music director for Elton's band. When we first met, I asked him if he wouldn't mind playing guitar for some of the

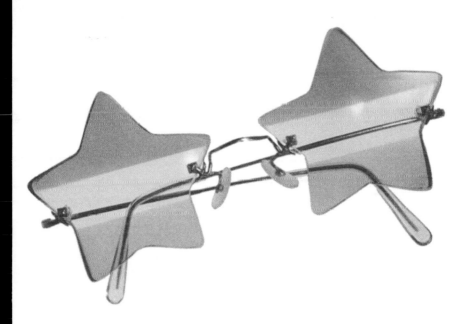

songs I was writing and recording. The work he ended up doing for me was, to say the least, magical. Davey even joined me on stage many times for various shows of my music I organized throughout the 1980s and 1990s. I am a very lucky man.

Then in 2005, that luck took a turn for the better. Davey asked me if I'd be interested in working as the stand-in for Elton for some rehearsals they were having in town since Elton's schedule was too packed for him to be available. "Wait, what? You want me to sit in *as* Elton and play piano and sing his parts?" I was no fool. I had to think about this. A millisecond later, I responded with a resounding "Yes!" and from that day on, I became known to the band as the "Surrogate Elton John," stepping into the most exciting "job" I ever had. Anyone who knew me growing up in Florida couldn't believe I was doing this!

Even my mother was impressed when I told her the news.

Friday

Adam—

You're not getting enough rest. You need to sleep at

Photo courtesy of the Elton John Archive.

least 8 hours a night! Drink some chamomile tea and
take an Advil PM.
Love,
Mom

Anyway, in the beginning of 2005, Sir Elton was preparing to do
a concert series to celebrate the thirtieth anniversary of the release
of his classic album *Captain Fantastic and the Brown Dirt Cowboy*. It
was one of my personal favorites, and Elton was planning to play
the entire album live in concert for the first time since 1975. Since
he hadn't played a lot of those songs for decades, I was brought on
board to help the band get up to speed in order to be ready for Elton.
As I drove home from my day job, songs like "Tower of Babel" and
"Better Off Dead" and "Curtains" blasted from my car stereo in order to refresh my memory as to how these songs were supposed to
sound. At times I felt like Rocky in training. I had to be "in shape" for
these rehearsals. They were going to be the most important rehearsals of my life.

It all ended up going so well that I was asked to join the band in
Boston and New York for their rehearsals there, and IF he were to
need it . . . to help the SIR himself with the piano parts for his very
own songs that he hadn't played or sung in ages. Can you believe it?
Was there a candid camera hiding somewhere? The trip to Boston
would mark the first time I was to be away from my new family unit.
But this was too big of a deal to pass up! Even Truman understood
that.

That first rehearsal in Boston began a few days before the shows
were to start. They rented out this beautiful old concert hall in the
middle of town. The eight-member choir, the band, the lighting
guys, film crew, sound guys—all of them were present as I ran several of the songs with everyone. When Elton arrived, I got up and
shook his hand.

He sat down at his grand piano while I sat directly across from
him at this little digital keyboard. The band began playing and Elton

was unsure of the first couple of chords to play. Everyone stopped, and Elton looked up at ME. I then proceeded to tell him what those chords were. *Hello?* I told Sir Elton John the chords he needed to know to play his song. *Seriously!* I want to write that again. I told Sir Elton John the chords he needed to know to play his song. Unreal. Anyway, after that whole session, my work there was theoretically over. I moved offstage and watched everything from one of the empty seats out in the audience.

When the rehearsal finished, to show their appreciation for my assistance, I was invited by Elton and his band to join the choir onstage for a series of sold-out shows at Boston's FleetCenter and New York's Madison Square Garden! The GARDEN! No shit? If you were to think biblically, Adam was heading back to the garden. This was to be a truly religious experience.

I've never known such a thrill as staring out INTO the audience FROM the stage of Madison Square Garden. I'll never forget it. Scott, one of my closest friends (*and director of my MTV video*), flew out from California to see it! Unfortunately, the choir members taught me their choreographed dance steps a day or so before the first show in Boston. By the time we were playing New York, I might have known all the right moves, but I was pretty sure I looked more like the character of Dancing Bear from *Captain Kangaroo* when I was doing anything other than singing onstage. In fact, after one of the New York shows, this nice couple from the audience found me outside and asked me if I had won that spot with the choir because I looked so out of place. OK. Fine. I could take the criticism. I was the one leaving with pictures of me and Elton up on the JumboTron in split screen singing the refrain from "Curtains" together.

"Tiny Dancer," I will never be.

Soon I was rehearsing with the band for other performances, sound checks, and television appearances, playing and singing all these songs I knew like the back of my hand! It was as though I was living a completely separate life in the eyes of my mother (*one that she seemed to ignore*).

When I returned home from that trip, I remember taking her for a ride to pick up my son from preschool. You know what she said to me? She said, "If Elton likes you so much, why doesn't he hire you for a full-time job?" That's it. No enthusiastic comments or congratulatory phrases about all I had been doing with him on tour. It's never good enough. I'm counting the days before she writes HIM.

My family had so much to be grateful for that Christmas in 2005! Even though I'm Jewish, we celebrate Christmas with a tree, presents, stockings, Santa Claus, etc. Besides, having my birthday on that day makes it an even happier time for all! That year, I received my first Christmas card from Sir Elton himself! The card probably cost more than our entire Christmas tree—and most of the presents underneath it.

I placed it carefully next to all the other Christmas cards hanging on the wall from friends, family, and, of course, my mother.

If you have a Christmas Tree, you can't leave lights
on when you're not home in case there's a short. It
could cause a fire. I saw it on CNN News! You have to
be careful about wiring. Some pictures I came across,
thought you'd like.
Love,
Mom

Sunday
Hello—
Thought I'd plan on coming out for 2 nights. Alone. I
need to have a little space from Nan for 2 days and I
want to see Truman. So, I'm planning on beginning
of March. Will discuss dates with you to see what's
convenient for you. I would stay at the hotel only
because I need very much to be alone or I will have to be
committed. My identity has been lost just when I almost
had one and I have to recover it.

Love,

Mom

P.S. Could you send Clive Davis, who is again head of
Arista Records, a sample of your music? He's 71 years
old now and Jewish and I think he would listen to you.
Try!

    Did you and Maria start your taxes?

Hang on here. Forget about my taxes and Clive Davis. Did my
mother just say that she needed a little space from HER mother?
That she lost her identity? Anyone care to join me in singing "The
Circle of Life"?

In 2006, my mother told me that she and my grandmother would
be moving to Los Angeles. Well, it's a free world. And they wanted to
be around family. I found my mother a room in some graduate student's apartment about twenty minutes away from our house. I also
found my grandmother an assisted-living home a short drive away,
as she was needing full-time assistance.

It was actually nice having them around for the birth of our second son in 2006. Maria and I decided to give him the most remark-
ably Jewish name in the galaxy: Marcello. Marcello is the complete
opposite of Truman. While Truman has dark hair and dark eyes
and looks exactly like my wife, Marcello is blond and blue-eyed and
looks exactly like my mother (sans the cane and the designer clothes).

As my sons grow to love each other as the brothers they are, my
mother's letters grow more and more peculiar.

Friday

Adam—

Check it out, Dude! (I like the way that guy Randy talks
on American Idol.) New York Life Insurance is hiring
people for various positions. I saw it in today's LA
Times. You should look into this. Their starting salary is
$34,000 a year.

Love,
Mom

Quoting Randy from *American Idol*? And hey! Sounds like she got herself a TV. Maybe I can send her a copy of my music video that was on MTV over twenty years ago THAT SHE TOLD ME SHE'D NEVER SEEN BEFORE! And regarding the $34,000 a year job: It was obviously time to make sure my résumé was up-to-date.

I might have pursued a career with New York Life Insurance, but, in 2007, I was offered the opportunity to arrange and conduct the sixty-plus–member Brooklyn Youth Chorus for Sir Elton John's sixtieth birthday concert at Madison Square Garden. I spent many evenings in front of a mirror practicing and getting myself together. This was a huge honor for me to step in as guest conductor, and an even greater responsibility compared to all the amazing things I was already happily doing for Elton and his band.

I searched all over for various live recordings of Elton to get an idea of how some of the songs might have changed over the years. I found a guy selling some great bootlegs on Craigslist. Bad move to share that find with my mother . . .

Tuesday
Adam—
Be careful about meeting people on "Craig's List." I
heard from CNN that there are a lot of criminals that
prey on people and they have met them to harm them
and steal from them. So be cautious!
Love,
Mom
P.S. Please don't go into Mexico because they are
kidnapping Americans and cutting off their heads!!

When I returned to Madison Square Garden for the big performance, it was my fourth time on that stage with my official Christmas card pal. The concert was simulcast on the Web around the world, so millions (*minus my mother, who doesn't own a computer*) would be able to watch me live my dream. Exhilarating beyond belief, this was one of the greatest moments of my life. I think I lost about ten pounds during those three hours under the lights. The choir got a kick out of my enthusiasm for the songs, and they did a wonderful job. Sometimes I take out the DVD of the concert and just keep it playing in the background (*ignored*) when my mother comes over.

The next few years found me starting this little blog I called "Please Don't Eat Sushi! Love, Mom!" Many people have asked me if my mother knows that I blog about her, and that I ended up writing this book about her letters. Sure she knows.

I think a part of her LIVES to be in the limelight. Until her big day comes, though, maybe she can pen an advice column for a newspaper or a magazine like . . . oh . . . *Parenting*. Imagine her dishing out good advice like:

February 23, 2009
Adam—
Watch Marcello as he puts things around his neck and he could choke himself! Also, make sure the front door is locked as anyone could come up and open the door.
    And, when you pick up Truman, make sure you get there early enough so you could get a parking spot.
    Why does Maria wait till I leave before she comes home? I never get to see her!
    Is it personal?
Love,
Mom

In a word, yes.
Could my mother be a spokesperson for the government health care system and any of its new suggested vaccinations?

Tuesday

Adam—

I got my flu shot today so if you don't hear from me by
tomorrow, you shouldn't take the shot! I feel fine so far,
but, you never know!

    Hope all is fine with you.

Love,

Mom

Maybe she could offer suggestions to people searching for exactly
the right gift for special occasions.

May 9, 2009

Adam—

For Mother's Day, I bought Maria a Ouija Board.

    I hope you both have fun using it.

Love,

Mom

I called my friend Ben the other day. He lives in Minnesota and
we don't get to speak to each other as often as we'd like. We both
have families and are very busy people, but we still manage to keep
in touch.

He mentioned that several months ago my mom sent him a letter.
"*She* sent *you* a letter?" I didn't even know she had his address. I'm not
sure why I acted surprised when I found out what the letter said. He
scanned it and e-mailed it to me. As I read it aloud for the first time
on my computer screen, I was propelled right back into junior high.

Benny—

Excuse the paper—I love the picture of your boys — They
are so beautiful—

Did you know Adam is selling his house? You should speak to him more often— He misses you—

Love—

Mrs. C

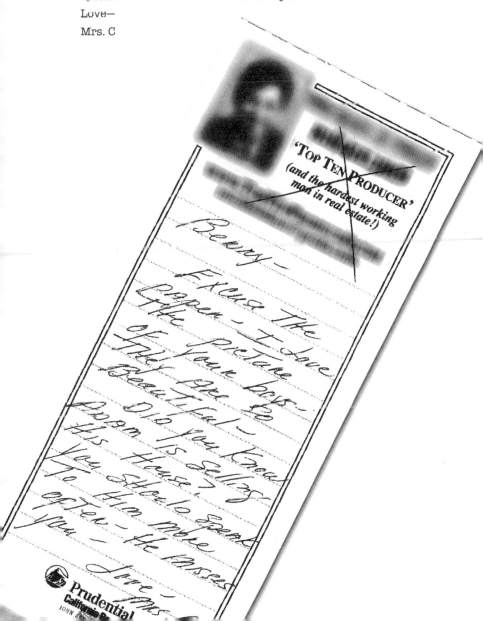

I couldn't imagine why my mother would feel so comfortable writing to Ben and telling him that he and I should speak more often. And that I MISSED him. What are we, ten years old? I know she means well, but really!

That said, couldn't my mother have found a decent piece of paper to write on? That one is courtesy of some Prudential Realtor known as the "hardest working man in real estate." Where does she dig this stuff up? Ironically, I believe my mother could be the mascot for all things "prudential."

And if you thought her being a "mother" to Ben was strange, wait until you read this:

Adam—
Encl. find a rough draft of the letter I wrote to the
President.
Mom

Dear Mr. President,
I think you will be one of the best Presidents that we
ever had.
    I worked for a bureaucracy as a social worker for
many years and I know how they work. Don't let the
"beasts" bother you. They want to keep things "Status
Quo" for their own benefit.
    Play it "close to the vest." You're the President—You
don't have to prove anything to anyone. You don't have
to go on the "Jay Leno" show or any other TV show.
You're above all that.
    Because you are such a "nice guy"—people will take
advantage of that. Just do what you do and keep away
from the "beasts."
    My cell # is: ███-███-████ & my address is: ████
███████ █████, ███ ████, ██ █████
Sincerely,
Joan

Adam—
Encl. Find a Rough
Draft of the Letter I
wrote To The President.
Mom

Dear Mr. President,
"I think you will be one
of the best Presidents that
we ever had.
I worked for a bureaucracy.
As A social worker For many
years, and I know how i behave
i work, and don't let the
bother you. they want For their
own benefit! STATus Quo For their
Things! i close to The best."
PLAYST you're President — you don't
have To prove anything To
anyone, You don't, i suppose To
put on the TV show, you're
already above all That.
i because you're pm Smarth.
A nicer guy — there will Take
advantage you. so that, just Do
without you, so and, keep busy
seem Like i beats,
i call it is!
Sincerely,
Jean [signature]

OH. MY. GOD.

Had she just finished watching *Omen III: The Final Conflict*? Who in heaven's name were these "beasts"? You just know the Secret Service will be tailing her ass (*and mine*) from this day forward as potential terrorists or just fucking loons. Then again, there is a small unrealistic part of me that hopes President Obama will take a moment out of his busy day leading the free world and all, and call my mother on the cell phone number she provided.

Yes, my mother longs to be the mother to all living things in lieu of being allowed to continue mothering me.

I grew up eating her spaghetti with ketchup until I left home for college. In my current life, when it comes to cooking, Maria is a chef extraordinaire! Her thirst for learning how to cook new and interesting foods has definitely helped me put on a few pounds. Recently, our family doctor told me that I was in good health, but that I should lose some weight and lower my cholesterol. Of course, word gets around when Maria tells HER mom, who tells MY mom, and then:

Saturday
Adam—
Please take care of your cholesterol! Keep taking those
pills from the health food store and call your doctor to
get it checked like you were supposed to do 3 weeks ago.
You can't wait till you lose more weight! And you can't
eat all the leftovers from the kids! That makes you gain
weight! You should join weight watchers. It's the best
program and you'd only have to go once a week. They
give you all good tips and if you were being weighed in
once a week, it would boost your confidence.
Do it for your kids. They need you to be in good health.

Love,

Mom

You can join on line and they will tell you where the
closest meeting to you at night is. (I would come over to
watch kids so you can go to a meeting.) It really would
enhance your good looks.

As we all get older, health does become a top priority. This one
almost got me to simultaneously quit smoking cigars AND become
an insomniac.

Wednesday

Adam—

I don't think there's anything wrong with you smoking
cigars. Look at George Burns. He lived a long life. Stop
letting Maria bully you around.

Love—

Mom

P.S. Get some rest!

Maria does NOT bully me around. She just tells me that cigars are
bad for me. I know that. George Burns probably knows that now. My
mother (*who smokes about two packs of cigarettes per day*) *should* know
that. But I can do no wrong.

Friday

Adam—

Annette (Maria's Mom) let a pair of strangers drive her
to your house! And you think I'm strange? She's a little
nutty herself! So don't always point at me and some
things I do. I never brought any strangers to your house.

Love,

Mom

Here's the story. During Annette's last visit to LA, she walked into a Starbucks to grab a hot coffee. It was dark outside already, and she didn't know when or where to catch the next bus back to our house. She then turned to, in her words, "a very nice Armenian couple," chugging down espressos at one of the tables there. Surprisingly, they didn't know the current local bus schedule and asked Annette where she needed to go. Since our house was only a few miles away, they offered to drive her to our front door. And she accepted.

I AM SURROUNDED BY CRAZY MOTHERS. And THEY are surrounded by strangers (*beasts?*) who at any time just may be trying to kill them.

Monday
Adam—
My roommate at this house I'm staying at just told me that she put poison down on her kitchen counters the other day. She said she saw a mouse there. I didn't know about it until just now and I'm the only one who cooks in the kitchen.

I told her if I drop dead in the next few days, my son will own her house and everything in it! I just wanted you to know.
Love,
Mom

Remember: TRUST NO ONE!

When it came to my career, this was the greatest advice I had ever received from anyone.

I'M not gonna tell her. YOU tell her!

Oct. 6, 2009

Adam—

I've got a great idea. I think you should call Seinfeld.
He's on Channel 13. Maybe he could put a character on
his show similar to you. Someone who's a struggling
musician doing all sorts of things to make a living. It
would be a great addition and I bet Seinfeld would <u>love</u>
it! He could even use your music in the episodes.

It was a brainstorm that just came to me.

Love,

Mom

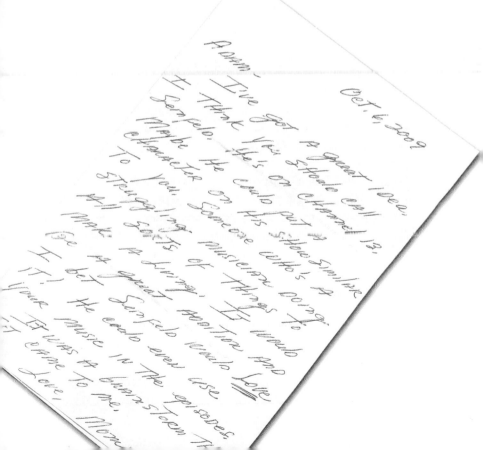

That's got to be one of the most classic displays of her "I-am-truly-unaware-of-anything-currently-going-on-in-this-world" syndrome. Other than the fact that *Seinfeld*'s been off the air for twelve years, it's a great idea. Thanks, Mom!

Sometimes I get worked up about all this craziness. But then I wake up and realize that's just the way things are. My mother loves her grandkids and they love their nanny. She says she loves me even though she seems to thrive on embarrassing me. I guess the bottom line is that she's my mother, and nothing can change that. My wife loves the idea that perhaps the damage she did (*is still doing*) to me with all these letters might be able to give back a little. (*You know, the book; the Adam's Mom line of pre-stamped envelopes; a fancy new line of pajamas to be worn outside…*)

My mother is in the process of moving (*again*). This time, she's moving out of the house of that lady who was allegedly trying to kill her with rat poison, and into a room in another woman's house located about ten minutes away from us. Of course, there IS a catch. The room will be vacant in one month from today. Because my mother burned her bridge with her current landlady, she was told she had to move out. NOW. Once again, it would appear that she is "homeless" for thirty days (*720 hours; 42,700 minutes*). With no money to stay at a hotel and no other friends or relatives in town, my mother will be crashing at our house for that period of time. I had to slip a few Lexapros into Maria's coffee yesterday morning. We're all a little stressed out about it right now and praying that her new arrangement doesn't fall through for some reason. If it does, get ready to hear about a new show, *Survivor: Adam's Mom,* that'll be filmed all across America, because she ain't staying here any longer. (*The tribe has spoken.*)

It's funny, but if you're around it for too long, you turn into a nut job, too. There have been times lately when I would hear the evening news report a tragedy in a land far, far away, and I'd be certain my wife and kids were there and badly injured. Just yesterday, I was sitting on the couch when I heard an ambulance in the distance and I was 100 percent positive that my family was en route to the nearest medical center. Some parents tell me this is pretty common. I think it's proof that what my mother has is contagious.

Though if there's one thing I've learned when it comes to this family, it's that no one is normal, and nothing is regular.

Mon.

Adam—

Grapes are very good for having bowel movements. I didn't see any grapes in your house!!

Mom

I just need to get ahold of myself. I want to stay sane and try to offer my boys the love and respect they deserve, while giving them the freedom they need to grow and learn for themselves. To me, that's what a parent should offer their children.

I'm on the precipice of turning fifty. Looking back thus far, I feel as though I've lived a pretty good life. I've bear-hugged Barry White, starred in an MTV video, sat in for Elton John at his band rehearsals, and I've got two of the best kids and the prettiest wife a guy could ever ask for, and a mother . . . and a mother . . .

Well, I knew it was sounding TOO good.

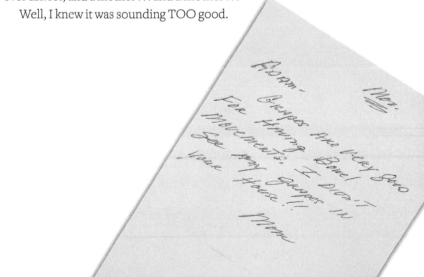

5.
P.S.

My name is Adam and I've got this collection of insanely inappropriate letters from my mother. Once upon a time, only a few people knew about them. Now a lot of people know about them. I'm not sure I'll ever fully understand what made me keep any of them in the first place. But in all honesty, I'm sure glad I did.

In closing, I'd now like to share with you a letter that I've been saving for this moment. It dates from 1987. I figured I had to present it here at the end so you, the reader, could better understand how dreadfully WRONG this is.

Sunday

Dear Adam—

After you left today, I've been thinking—

Why can't you & I share an apt. in LA together—I'll get a job out there and I could pay half the rent?

We could get a 2-BR apt. so we each could have our own BR—I would be happy & you could pursue your career!

I would be so happy to get away from Miami and being near you.

If you don't want to—I won't—But—would you think about it?

Love,

Mom

P.S. It would cut down a lot of my expenses so that I would be able to give you more money—It would cut down my: utilities

       phone

       airfare

I'd rather give the money to you.

Love,
Mom

6.

Here Comes the Son

It's such a beautiful spring day here in Southern California. You can make out the shapes of all the clouds in the sky. There's a faint breeze in the air, and it's curiously humid out. I can hear that familiar sound of happy children playing outside from where I'm sitting just in front of Truman's elementary school. Since I'm a few hours early, I'm just hanging out in my car with the top down and soaking up some last-minute . . . hey, there he is! I can see him in the school yard running around with all his little friends and . . .

Hey, what's my mother doing here?

Mom?

Mom!

She can't hear me.

Mom!

Yo!

    I wonder what she's . . .

    Wait!

    Oh, no.

    Why is she carrying a . . .

Oh my God!
OH MY GOD!
No!
Mommmmmmmmmmm!!!!!!
NO!!!!!
PUT.
THE.
SWEATER.
DOWN!
NOOOOOOOOOOOOOOO!!!!!
RUN, TRUMAN!
RRRRRRRUUUUUUUUUUUNNNNNNNNNN!
RRRRRRRRRRRRRRRRUUUUUUUUNNNNN!

Maria: Honey, are you alright?
Adam: (*sitting up, rubbing eyes*) Sorry, babe. It was
that damn nightmare again.

The End.

Acknowledgments

Scott Alexander, Dave Lesser, Ben Bejar, Mike Huckman, and John Klekamp. I truly couldn't have done this without you. My love and thanks!

My grandmother Natalie for helping to foster my mother's personality.

My wife, Maria, who is a crazy-mother kindred spirit and the love of my life.

My boys, Truman and Marcello, who probably have this in their genes. There is no antibody.

My mother-in-law, Annette, who should have a part in the movie, if there ever is one.

Me (*if I may*) for having the foresight to know I needed to save my mother's letters.

My father, Eliot . . . look, if you're hiding somewhere, please come out. I forgive you.

And to my mother—I kept this collection hidden for far too long. You are a wonderful human being and grandmother to my children, and I want you to know that you have made me a proud son and a faithful father.

I feel lucky that I'm the one who gets to call you Mom.

Wait a minute. Who am I kidding? She probably won't ever read this book.

Never mind.

Special thanks also go to: Paul Kaufman; and to Paul Haas, Zachary Druker, and Jay Mandel from WME; Todd Cohen and Carolyn Bernstein from Reveille; Jack Black at Electric Dynamite; and, my publisher David Cashion, for listening to my mother when I didn't.

About the Author

Adam works as a professional composer and singer/songwriter who is employed as the official "Surrogate Elton John." Adam sits in as Elton John, playing piano and singing while rehearsing the Elton John Band for various shows, sound checks, and appearances.

He is married to a fearless woman. They have two beautiful boys and reside in Los Angeles, California. Adam's mom lives about twenty minutes away, and since he will not respond to various inappropriate phone messages, she still writes Adam at least four times a month.

The Author's Mom

Adam's mom has lived in Miami; New York City; Syracuse; Las Vegas; Houston; Boston; and Princeton, South Orange, Wayne, and Bayonne, New Jersey. She currently resides in Los Angeles but will most likely be moving again soon.

She unconditionally loves her son and is a huge advocate of the United States Postal Service.